Kelsey Elam

IVY PRESS

First published in the UK in 2016 by
Ivy Press
Ovest House, 58 West Street
Brighton BN1 2RA, UK
www.quartoknows.com

Copyright © The Ivy Press Ltd 2016

All rights reserved. No part of this publication
may be reproduced or transmitted in any form
by any means, electronic or mechanical, including
photocopying, recording or by any information
storage-and-retrieval system, without written
permission from the copyright holder.

British Library Cataloguing-in-Publication Data
A CIP catalogue record for this book is available
from the British Library.

ISBN: 978-1-78240-308-1

This book was conceived, designed, and produced by

Ivy Press

Publisher Susan Kelly
Creative Director Michael Whitehead
Art Director Wayne Blades
Commissioning Editor Sophie Collins
Editorial Director Tom Kitch
Senior Project Editor Caroline Earle
Book Design and Illustration Evelin Kasikov
Photographer Neal Grundy

Typeset in Gotham

Printed and bound in China

10 9 8 7 6 5 4 3 2

INTRODUCTION
4

THE ANATOMY OF A FLOWER
6

100 PAPER FLOWERS
8

Introduction

Making paper flowers is a wonderful way to be creative while also exploring one of the glories of the natural world. Anyone can enjoy this creative and beautiful hobby, and you can share the joy with friends and family. Handmade bouquets make wonderful presents, keepsakes, and decorations.

I began creating paper flowers because I wanted a personal way to make gifts for loved ones. I found that I enjoyed capturing the essence of a bloom in paper, recreating nature's awe-inspiring spectrum of color and detail. Every paper flower that I create is made with love, and also with attention to the color and pattern. I like to exaggerate my favorite traits and features in my flowers, and I encourage you to do the same.

Paper flowers can look amazingly realistic, and they are a beautiful way to brighten up your home or to decorate for a wedding, christening, or other celebration. I often use them to make my gift-wrapping extra-special. Each bloom is delicately handcrafted from hand-dyed, bleached, and painted tissue paper as well as from other miscellaneous papers and fibers, which can be incorporated into the design to add interesting effects and textures. Most papers used are upcycled from gift wrapping and packing material. As for tools, you will already have most of what you need to hand. If not, then they are readily available at craft stores or online.

This book includes a hundred of my favorite flowers along with four flower projects. It is divided into three sections: a beautiful gallery, a techniques section, and a templates section. Enjoy browsing through the gallery and choosing the flower you want to make. Each flower has a list of materials, and then a list of the techniques used to make it. You will find the precise instructions for each method in the techniques chapter. As you become more adept at making the flowers, you will be able to see at a glance what stages or techniques are used, and can experiment with different colors, patterns, and arrangements. Let your imagination run free.

Kelsey Elam

How to use this book

Gallery

One hundred flowers shown in all their glory, as well as four special projects, with a full-page image. Each flower comes with a list of the materials needed to make it, and the techniques used, listed in the order that you need them. Turn to the templates chapter for the right pattern, and the techniques section for the detailed instructions.

Techniques

The techniques are organized into 13 general categories, from paper painting to attaching leaves. Each category includes easy-to-follow instructions to take you through every step of the process required for the flower you are making.

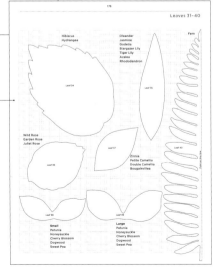

Templates

At the back of the book you will find all the templates you need for the leaves, petals, and other flower parts. Each template is shown actual size and numbered; you'll find the relevant pattern and page number for the template required in the list of materials on the flower pages.

The Anatomy of a Flower

Paper flowers are made of layers beginning at the very center of the flower and working down to the bottom of the stem. There are several techniques used to create each part of a paper flower, which, when used in different combinations, can be used to make many varieties of flowers.

Center and stamen

Most paper flowers begin with the center or stamen. Attached directly to the floral wire stem, centers can be created from tissue or crepe paper fringe, modeling clay with the stem pressed into the wet clay, paper-covered cotton balls, paper-covered cotton swabs cut in half and taped to the floral wire, or ready-made pips.

Petals

Created from tissue or crepe paper, petals can be altered in any way you can imagine for texture and color variations. They are usually created by cutting individual petal shapes or you can make "continuous" petals, which remain connected at the bottom of the paper. Petals can be scrunched, pleated, twisted, curled, and cupped to mimic natural petal shapes.

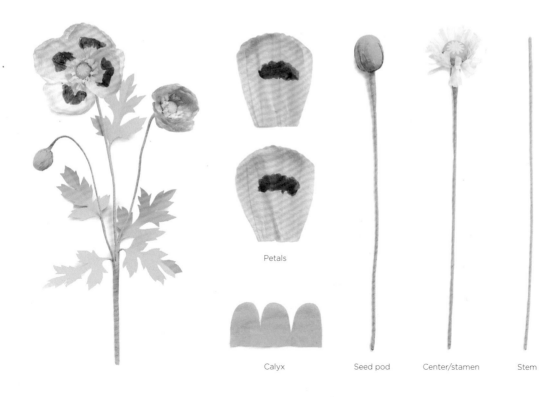

Petals

Calyx

Seed pod

Center/stamen

Stem

Leaf

Calyx and sepals

The calyx is formed by sepal pieces directly below the flower's petals. The calyx is an optional element used to create a more detailed and lifelike bloom.

Leaves

Leaves can be made from tissue paper or card stock. They can be attached directly to the main stem of the flower or can have their own stems. Some foliage varieties have added detailing created with paint, ink, or a glossy finishing coat.

Tendrils

Tendrils add a fun element to several of the plant varieties in this book, and can be manipulated to show different effects from tight, even corkscrew curls to wild curls that point in all directions.

Berries, buds, and seedpods

Berries, buds, and seedpods are created from modeling clay, cotton balls, or paper, and add visual interest to any flower stem or arrangement. Buds and seedpods are optional, but add a lifelike quality to your paper creations.

Stems

Stems are the flowers' support system. They are made from floral wire in various gauges and covered with tissue paper strips or floral tape.

Tendril   Leaf   Bud   Petals

100
Paper
Flowers

Geranium

YOU WILL NEED:

- Eight pink single pip stamens on eight 4½in (11cm), 22-gauge (0.65mm) wire stems
- Five 4½in (11cm), 22-gauge (0.65mm) wires for leaf stems
- One 12in (30cm), 18-gauge (1mm) wire for main stem
- Green tissue paper: one 15 x ½in (38 x 1.2cm) strip for main stem, thirteen 6 x ½in (15 x 1.2cm) strips for small stems
- Red tissue paper: 16 petal pieces, 2 petal pieces per small bloom (petal pattern 48, p187)
- Green card stock: 5 leaves (leaf patterns 15 and 17, p171)

TECHNIQUES:

- **5:** Making centers—single pip stamen (position the stamen with the bulbous part directly above the wire, attaching the entire length of the white filament to the wire)
- **4:** Petal styling—pinching (attach the petals at the end of the wire, situated around the bottom of the pip stamen)
- **3:** Paper painting—painting card stock leaves
- **7:** Making leaves—card stock leaves
- **10:** Covering stems
- **12:** Attaching extra stems—cluster (create two clusters—a larger cluster of five blooms at the top of the main wire and a smaller cluster of three blooms attached approximately 4in (10cm) from the top of the main stem)
- **13:** Styling leaves and stems

Hydrangea

YOU WILL NEED:

- Ten light blue single pip stamens on ten 4½in (11cm), 22-gauge (0.65mm) wire stems
- Two 4½in (11cm), 22-gauge (0.65mm) wires for leaf stems
- One 9in (23cm), 18-gauge (1mm) wire for main stem
- Green tissue paper: one 12 x ½in (30 x 1.2cm) strip for main stem, twelve 6 x ½in (15 x 1.2cm) strips for small stems
- Teal blue tissue paper: 20 petal pieces, 2 petal pieces per small bloom (petal pattern 48, p187)
- Green card stock: 2 leaves (leaf pattern 34, p175)

TECHNIQUES:

- **5:** Making centers—single pip stamen (position the stamen with the bulbous part directly above the wire, attaching the entire length of the white filament to the wire)
- **4:** Petal styling—pinching (attach the petals at end of the wire, situated around the bottom of the pip stamen)
- **7:** Making leaves—card stock leaves
- **10:** Covering stems
- **12:** Attaching extra stems—cluster
- **13:** Styling leaves and stems

Rhododendron

YOU WILL NEED:

- Six yellow triple pip stamens on six 4½in (11cm), 20-gauge (0.8mm) wire stems
- Six 4½in (11cm), 20-gauge (0.8mm) wires for leaf stems
- One 9in (23cm), 18-gauge (1mm) wire for main stem
- Green tissue paper: one 12 x ½in (30 x 1.2cm) strip for main stem, twelve 6 x ½in (15 x 1.2cm) strips for small stems
- Light blue tissue paper dipped in light blue dye: 48 petal pieces, 4 double petals per small bloom (petal pattern 47, p187)
- Green card stock: 6 leaves (leaf pattern 35, p175)

TECHNIQUES:

- **1:** Paper dyeing—dyeing colored tissue paper
- **5:** Making centers—multiple pip stamen
- **4:** Petal styling—scrunching
- **8:** Attaching petals—double petals (arrange 4 double petals evenly around each of the 6 centers to create the small blooms)
- **7:** Making leaves—card stock leaves
- **10:** Covering stems
- **12:** Attaching extra stems—cluster (attach all 6 leaves directly below the cluster of blooms, joining each stem at the same height)
- **13:** Styling leaves and stems

Azalea

YOU WILL NEED:

- Six light yellow triple pip stamens on six 4½in (11cm), 20-gauge (0.8mm) wire stems
- Three 4½in (11cm), 20-gauge (0.8mm) wires for leaf stems
- One 9in (23cm), 18-gauge (1mm) wire for main stem
- Light green tissue paper: one 12 x ½in (30 x 1.2cm) strip for main stem, nine 6 x ½in (15 x 1.2cm) strips for small stems
- Peach tissue paper dipped in bleach: 24 petal pieces, 4 petal pieces per small bloom (petal pattern 47, p187)
- Light green card stock: 3 leaves (leaf pattern 35, p175)

TECHNIQUES:

- **2**: Paper bleaching
- **5**: Making centers—multiple pip stamen
- **4**: Petal styling—scrunching
- **8**: Attaching petals—single petals
- **10**: Covering stems
- **7**: Making leaves—card stock leaves
- **12**: Attaching extra stems—cluster
- **13**: Styling leaves and stems

Angel Cheeks Pom Peony

YOU WILL NEED:

- One 9in (23cm), 18-gauge (1mm) wire stem
- Two 4½in (11cm), 20-gauge (0.8mm) wires for leaf stems
- Light green tissue paper: one 12 x ½in (30 x 1.2cm) strip for stem, two 6 x ½in (15 x 1.2cm) strips for leaf stems
- White tissue paper: 4 fringed petal pieces for the center (petal pattern 19, p183)
- Yellow tissue paper: 1 fringed petal piece for center (petal pattern 19, p183)
- Yellow tissue paper painted with red stripes: 1 fringed petal piece for center (petal pattern 19, p183)
- Pale pink tissue paper: 10 small petals and 10 large petals paired to create 5 double petals of each size (petal patterns 16 and 18, p182)
- Light green card stock: 2 leaves (leaf patterns 45 and 46, p176)

TECHNIQUES:

- **3:** Paper painting—acrylic craft paint stripes for one yellow tissue paper piece
- **1:** Paper dyeing—using water for all other petals
- **4:** Petal styling—scrunching for fringed center petals and pleating for pink petals
- **8:** Attaching petals—continuous petals for fringed center petals (attach all six petal pieces allowing the color placement to be random)
- **9:** Attaching petals—double petals for pink petals (arrange the small double petals evenly around the fringe petal center, then add the large double petals evenly)
- **10:** Covering stems
- **7:** Making leaves—card stock leaves
- **12:** Attaching extra stems—single bloom
- **13:** Styling leaves and stems

Pink Hawaiian Charm Peony

YOU WILL NEED:

- One triple cotton swab center on 9in (23cm), 18-gauge (1mm) wire stem
- Two 4½in (11cm), 20-gauge (0.8mm) wires for leaf stems
- Light green tissue paper: three 2 x 2in (5 x 5cm) pieces for cotton swab centers, one 12 x ½in (30 x 1.2cm) strip for stem, two 6 x ½in (15 x 1.2cm) strips for leaf stems
- Golden yellow tissue paper: one 3 x 5in (7.5 x 12cm) piece for medium fringed center
- Hot pink tissue paper dipped in bleach: 10 small petals and 10 large petals paired to create 5 double petals of each size (petal patterns 16 and 18, p182)
- Light green card stock: 2 leaves (leaf patterns 45 and 46, p176)

TECHNIQUES:

- **2:** Paper bleaching—dipped
- **5:** Making centers—triple cotton swab center
- **3:** Paper painting—painting center accents
- **5:** Making centers—medium fringe center
- **4:** Petal styling—scrunching and pleating for all petals
- **8:** Attaching petals—double petals (arrange the small double petals evenly around the fringed center, then add the large double petals evenly)
- **7:** Making leaves—card stock leaves
- **10:** Covering stems
- **12:** Attaching extra stems—single bloom
- **13:** Styling leaves and stems

Misaka Itoh Peony

YOU WILL NEED:

- One triple cotton swab center on 9in (23cm), 18-gauge (1mm) wire stem
- Two 4½in (11cm), 20-gauge (0.8mm) wires for leaf stems
- Light green tissue paper: three 2 x 2in (5 x 5cm) pieces for cotton swab centers, one 12 x ½in (30 x 1.2cm) strip for stem, two 6 x ½in (15 x 1.2cm) strips for leaf stems
- Golden yellow tissue paper: one 3 x 5in (7.5 x 12cm) piece for medium fringed center
- Pale yellow tissue paper dipped in water: 10 small petals, 10 medium petals, and 10 large petals paired to create 5 double petals of each size (petal patterns 16, 17, and 18, p182)
- Light green card stock: 2 leaves (leaf patterns 45 and 46, p176)

TECHNIQUES:

- **3:** Paper painting—painting individual petals
- **3:** Paper painting—painting center accents
- **5:** Making centers—triple cotton swab center
- **5:** Making centers—medium fringe center
- **4:** Petal styling—scrunching and pleating for all petals
- **8:** Attaching petals—double petals (arrange the small double petals evenly around the fringed center, then add the medium double petals, followed by attaching the large double petals evenly)
- **7:** Making leaves—card stock leaves
- **10:** Covering stems
- **12:** Attaching extra stems—single bloom
- **13:** Styling leaves and stems

Dinnerplate Dahlia

YOU WILL NEED:

- One 9in (23cm), 18-gauge (1mm) wire stem
- Two 4½in (11cm), 20-gauge (0.8mm) wires for leaf stems
- Light green tissue paper: one 12 x ½in (30 x 1.2cm) strip for stem, two 6 x ½in (15 x 1.2cm) strips for leaf stem
- Golden yellow or light orange tissue paper: one 3 x 10in (7.5 x 25cm) piece for large fringed center
- Black tissue paper, white tissue paper with fuchsia painted stripes, or peach tissue paper dipped in bleach: 6 to 8 petal pieces (petal pattern 54, p189)
- Light green card stock: 2 leaves (leaf pattern 42, p176)

TECHNIQUES:

- **1:** Paper dyeing—using water (for the black dahlia)
- **2:** Paper bleaching—dipped (for the peach dahlia)
- **3:** Paper painting—watercolor or acrylic ink stripes (for the white dahlia with fuchsia painted stripes)
- **5:** Making centers—large fringe center
- **4:** Petal styling—scrunching
- **8:** Attaching petals—continuous petals (create three or four layers of random but evenly placed petals, working with two petal pieces per layer)
- **7:** Making leaves—card stock leaves
- **10:** Covering stems
- **12:** Attaching extra stems—single bloom
- **13:** Styling leaves and stems

Double Dahlia

YOU WILL NEED:

- Two 9in (23cm), 20-gauge (0.8mm) wire stem
- One 4½in (11cm), 20-gauge (0.8mm) wire for leaf stem
- Green tissue paper: two 12 x ½in (30 x 1.2cm) strips for stems, one 6 x ½in (15 x 1.2cm) strip for leaf stem
- Yellow tissue paper: two 3 x 5in (7.5 x 12cm) pieces for 2 medium fringed centers
- White tissue paper with red painted stripes: 8 small petal pieces, 4 pieces per bloom, and 4 large petal pieces for the larger bloom (petal patterns 49 and 50, p188)
- Green card stock: 1 leaf (leaf pattern 42, p176)

TECHNIQUES:

- **3:** Paper painting—acrylic craft paint stripes
- **5:** Making centers—medium fringe center
- **4:** Petal styling—scrunching
- **8:** Attaching petals—continuous petals (arrange four small petal pieces evenly around each fringe center, then add all four large petal pieces to one bloom to create one larger bloom and one smaller bloom)
- **7:** Making leaves—card stock leaves
- **10:** Covering stems
- **12:** Attaching extra stems—single bloom (join the two single blooms together allowing the larger bloom to rise slightly above the smaller bloom)
- **13:** Styling leaves and stems

Chrysanthemum

YOU WILL NEED:

- One 9in (23cm), 20-gauge (0.8mm) wire stem
- Two 4½in (11cm), 20-gauge (0.8mm) wires for leaf stems
- Green tissue paper: one 12 x ½in (30 x 1.2cm) strip for stem, two 6 x ½in (15 x 1.2cm) strips for leaf stem
- Teal tissue paper: 4 small petal pieces (petal pattern 53, p188)
- Teal tissue paper dipped in bleach: 4 large petal pieces (petal pattern 49, p188)
- Green card stock: 2 leaves (leaf patterns 27 and 28, p173)

TECHNIQUES:

- **2:** Paper bleaching—dipped
- **4:** Petal styling—scrunching
- **8:** Attaching petals—continuous petals (attach all 4 small petal pieces evenly around the wire stem, then arrange the 4 large petal pieces evenly around the inner petals)
- **7:** Making leaves—card stock leaves
- **10:** Covering stems
- **12:** Attaching extra stems—single bloom
- **13:** Styling leaves and stems

Thistle

YOU WILL NEED:

- One 9in (23cm), 20-gauge (0.8mm) wire stem
- Three 4½in (11cm), 22-gauge (0.65mm) wires for leaf stems
- Light green tissue paper: one 12 x ½in (30 x 1.2cm) strip for main stem, three 6 x ½in (15 x 1.2cm) strips for leaf stems
- Light purple tissue paper: one 3 x 10in (7.5 x 25cm) piece for large fringed center to form bloom (petal pattern 41, p187)
- Light green card stock: 3 leaves (leaf patterns 27 and 28, p173)

TECHNIQUES:

- **5:** Making centers—large fringe center (the bloom is created by simply creating a fringed center)
- **7:** Making leaves—card stock leaves
- **10:** Covering stems
- **12:** Attaching extra stems—single bloom
- **13:** Styling leaves and stems

Cornflower

YOU WILL NEED:

- Two 9in (23cm), 22-gauge (0.65mm) wire stems
- Green tissue paper: two 12 x ½in (30 x 1.2cm) strips for stems and 4 leaves (leaf patterns 29 and 30, p173)
- Blue tissue paper: 5 petal pieces, 3 pieces for the larger bloom and 2 pieces for the smaller bloom (petal pattern 40, p187)

TECHNIQUES:

- **4:** Petal styling—scrunching
- **8:** Attaching petals—continuous petals (arrange three pieces for the larger bloom and two pieces for the smaller bloom)
- **7:** Making leaves—small tissue paper leaves
- **10:** Covering stems
- **11:** Attaching leaves—tissue paper leaves
- **12:** Attaching extra stems—single bloom (join the two single blooms together allowing the larger bloom to rise slightly above the smaller bloom)
- **13:** Styling leaves and stems

Carnation

YOU WILL NEED:

- Two 9in (23cm), 22-gauge (0.65mm) wire stems
- Green tissue paper: two 12 x ½in (30 x 1.2cm) strips for stems and 8 leaves (leaf patterns 29 and 30, p173)
- Hot pink tissue paper with bleached stripes: 8 petal pieces, 5 pieces for the larger bloom and 3 pieces for the smaller bloom (petal pattern 41, p187)

TECHNIQUES:

- **2:** Paper bleaching—stripes
- **4:** Petal styling—scrunching
- **8:** Attaching petals—continuous petals (arrange 5 pieces for the larger bloom and 3 pieces for the smaller bloom)
- **7:** Making leaves—small tissue paper leaves
- **10:** Covering stems
- **11:** Attaching leaves—tissue paper leaves
- **12:** Attaching extra stems—single bloom (join the two single blooms together, allowing the larger bloom to rise slightly above the smaller bloom)
- **13:** Styling leaves and stems

Marigold

YOU WILL NEED:

- Three 9in (23cm), 22-gauge (0.65mm) wire stems for blooms
- Two 4½in (11cm), 22-gauge (0.65mm) wires for leaf stems
- Green tissue paper: three 12 x ½in (30 x 1.2cm) strips for stems and two 6 x ½in (15 x 1.2cm) strips for leaf stems
- Golden yellow tissue paper with burgundy painted stripes: 15 petal pieces, 5 pieces per bloom (petal pattern 40, p187)
- Green card stock: 2 leaves (leaf pattern 25, p173)

TECHNIQUES:

- **3:** Paper painting—watercolor or acrylic ink stripes
- **4:** Petal styling—scrunching
- **8:** Attaching petals—continuous petals (attach 5 petal pieces for each bloom)
- **7:** Making leaves—card stock leaves
- **10:** Covering stems
- **12:** Attaching extra stems—single bloom (join two of the single blooms together allowing one bloom to rise slightly above the other bloom, then add the third bloom slightly below the first two)
- **13:** Styling leaves and stems

Sweet Pea

YOU WILL NEED:

- Three to five 4½in (11cm), 22-gauge (0.65mm) wire stems for blooms
- Three 9in (23cm), 22-gauge (0.65mm) wire stems for tendrils
- One 18in (46cm), 18-gauge (1mm) wire for main stem
- Light green tissue paper: one 20 x ½in (50 x 1.2cm) strip for main stem, three to five 6 x ½in (15 x 1.2cm) strips for smaller stems, three 12 x ½in (30 x 1.2cm) strips for tendril stems, and 2 leaf pieces (leaf patterns 38 and 39, p175)
- Light purple tissue paper dipped in bleach: 6–10 petal pieces to create 3–5 double petals (petal pattern 34, p185)

TECHNIQUES:

- **2:** Paper bleaching—dipped
- **4:** Petal styling—scrunching
- **8:** Attaching petals—continuous petals (before attaching the petals to the wire stems, divide the petals into pairs, then layer and tack two petal pieces together with a small line of glue at the bottom of the petals)
- **4:** Petal styling—rolled curling (use fingers then roll the outer petals away from the inner petals)
- **7:** Making leaves—small tissue paper leaves
- **10:** Covering stems
- **11:** Attaching leaves—tissue paper leaves
- **12:** Attaching extra stems—tendrils and spike (begin by attaching one tendril to the top of the main wire, then arrange the blooms evenly in a row down the main stem, followed by the last two tendrils)
- **13:** Styling leaves and stems

Lupine

YOU WILL NEED:

- Sixteen 4½in (11cm), 22-gauge (0.65mm) wire stems for blooms
- Two 4½in (11cm), 22-gauge (0.65mm) wires for leaf stems
- One 18in (46cm), 18-gauge (1mm) wire for main stem
- Light green tissue paper: one 20 x ½in (50 x 1.2cm) strip for main stem, eighteen 6 x ½in (15 x 1.2cm) strips for small stems
- White tissue paper: 16 petal pieces (petal pattern 33, p185)
- Dark blue tissue paper: 16 petal pieces (petal pattern 33, p185)
- Light green card stock: 2 leaves (leaf pattern 26, p173)

TECHNIQUES:

- **4:** Petal styling—scrunching
- **8:** Attaching petals—continuous petals (before attaching the petals to the wire stems, layer the white petal pieces on top of the blue petal pieces and tack the two petal pieces together with a small line of glue at the bottom of the petals)
- **7:** Making leaves—card stock leaves
- **10:** Covering stems
- **12:** Attaching extra stems—spike
- **13:** Styling leaves and stems

Jasmine

YOU WILL NEED:

- Six yellow single pip stamens on six 4½in (11cm), 22-gauge (0.65mm) wire stems
- Three 4½in (11cm), 22-gauge (0.65mm) wire stems for buds
- Five 4½in (11cm), 22-gauge (0.65mm) wires for leaf stems
- One 9in (23cm), 18-gauge (1mm) wire for main stem
- Green tissue paper: one 12 x ½in (30 x 1.2cm) strip for main stem, fourteen 6 x ½in (15 x 1.2cm) strips for small stems
- Light pink tissue paper: three 1 x 10in (2.5 x 25cm) strips for buds
- White tissue paper dyed pink: 6 petal pieces, 1 piece per small bloom (petal pattern 35, p186)
- Green card stock: 5 leaves (leaf pattern 35, p175)

TECHNIQUES:

- **1:** Paper dyeing—dyeing white tissue paper
- **5:** Making centers—single pip stamen
- **4:** Petal styling—scrunching
- **8:** Attaching petals—continuous petals
- **6:** Making berries and buds—rolled paper buds
- **7:** Making leaves—card stock leaves
- **10:** Covering stems
- **12:** Attaching extra stems—spike (attach the blooms, buds, and leaves in random order along the length of the main stem)
- **13:** Styling leaves and stems

Borage

YOU WILL NEED:

- Six single cotton swab centers on six 4½in (11cm), 22-gauge (0.65mm) wire stems
- Three 4½in (11cm), 22-gauge (0.65mm) wires for leaf stems
- One 9in (23cm), 18-gauge (1mm) wire for main stem
- Green tissue paper: one 12 x ½in (30 x 1.2cm) strip for main stem, nine 6 x ½in (15 x 1.2cm) strips for small stems, 6 calyx pieces (cuff pattern 3, p189)
- White tissue paper: six 2 x 2in (5 x 5cm) pieces for cotton swab centers
- Blue tissue paper: 6 petal pieces, 1 piece per small bloom (petal pattern 35, p186)
- Green card stock: 3 leaves (leaf pattern 8, p169)

TECHNIQUES:

- **5:** Making centers—single cotton swab center
- **3:** Paper painting—painting center accents
- **4:** Petal styling—scrunching
- **8:** Attaching petals—continuous petals
- **9:** Attaching the calyx
- **10:** Covering stems
- **7:** Making leaves—card stock leaves
- **12:** Attaching extra stems—cluster
- **13:** Styling leaves and stems

Allium

YOU WILL NEED:

- Ten lavender single pip stamens on ten 4½in (11cm), 22-gauge (0.65mm) wire stems
- One 9in (23cm), 18-gauge (1mm) wire for main stem
- Light green tissue paper: one 12 x ½in (30 x 1.2cm) strip for main stem, ten 6 x ½in (15 x 1.2cm) strips for small stems
- Light purple tissue paper dipped in purple dye: 20 petal pieces, 2 pieces per small bloom (petal pattern 35, p186)
- Light green card stock: 2 leaves (leaf pattern 14, p170)

TECHNIQUES:

- **1**: Paper dyeing—colored tissue paper
- **5**: Making centers—pip stamen centers
- **4**: Petal styling—scrunching
- **8**: Attaching petals—continuous petals (arrange two petal pieces evenly around each stamen center)
- **10**: Covering stems
- **7**: Making leaves—card stock leaves
- **11**: Attaching leaves—card stock leaves
- **12**: Attaching extra stems—cluster
- **13**: Styling leaves and stems

Fern

YOU WILL NEED:

- One 15in (38cm), 20-gauge (0.8mm) wire stem
- Light green tissue paper: one 20 x ½in (50 x 1.2cm) strip for stem
- Light green card stock: 1 leaf (leaf pattern 40, p175)

TECHNIQUES:

- **7:** Making leaves—card stock leaves and pronounced veins
- **10:** Covering stems
- **13:** Styling leaves and stems

Dusty Miller

YOU WILL NEED:

- One 12in (30cm), 20-gauge (0.8mm) wire stem
- Sage green tissue paper: one 15 x ½in (38 x 1.2cm) strip for stem
- Sage green or light gray card stock: 1 leaf (leaf pattern 9, p169)

TECHNIQUES:

- **3:** Paper painting—painting card stock leaves
- **7:** Making leaves—card stock leaves and pronounced veins
- **10:** Covering stems
- **13:** Styling leaves and stems

Anthurium Lily

YOU WILL NEED:

- One clay oblong center on a 9in (23cm), 20-gauge (0.8mm) wire stem
- Light green tissue paper: one 12 x ½in (30 x 1.2cm) strip for stem
- Light yellow tissue paper: one 2 x 2in (5 x 5cm) piece for center
- Red card stock: 1 petal (petal pattern 1, p178)

TECHNIQUES:

- **5**: Making centers—oblong clay center
- **3**: Paper painting—glossy card stock leaves
- **7**: Making leaves—card stock leaves (for the red petals)
- **4**: Petal styling—pinching (cut the hole approximately ½in (1.2cm) in from the "V" of the petal lobes)
- **10**: Covering stems
- **12**: Attaching extra stems—single bloom
- **13**: Styling leaves and stems

Ranunculus

YOU WILL NEED:

- One clay oblong center on a 9in (23cm), 20-gauge (0.8mm) wire stem
- Two 4½in (11cm), 22-gauge (0.65mm) wires for leaf stems
- Light green tissue paper: one 2 x 2in (5 x 5cm) piece for clay center, one 12 x ½in (30 x 1.2cm) strip for stem, two 6 x ½in (15 x 1.2cm) strips for leaf stems, 3 petal pieces (petal pattern 2, p179)
- Hot pink, orange, golden yellow, or light yellow tissue paper dipped in water: 3–5 petal pieces; more pieces will create larger bloom (petal pattern 2, p179)
- Light green card stock: 2 leaves (leaf patterns 32 and 33, p174)

TECHNIQUES:

- **1:** Paper dyeing—using water
- **5:** Making centers—oblong clay center
- **3:** Paper painting—painting center accents
- **4:** Petal styling—scrunching
- **8:** Attaching petals—continuous petals (arrange the first two green petal pieces evenly around the center, then add the next petal piece in the color of your choice, followed by the last green petal, then add the rest of the petals; add as many or few as you prefer, staggering the petals of each layer)
- **7:** Making leaves—card stock leaves
- **10:** Covering stems
- **12:** Attaching extra stems—single bloom
- **13:** Styling leaves and stems

Double Camellia

YOU WILL NEED:

- One 9in (23cm), 20-gauge (0.8mm) wire stem
- Three 4½in (11cm), 20-gauge (0.8mm) wires for leaf stems
- Light green tissue paper: one 12 x ½in (30 x 1.2cm) strip for main stem, three 6 x ½in (15 x 1.2cm) strips for small stems
- Light yellow tissue paper: one 3 x 5in (7.5 x 12cm) piece for medium fringed center
- Red tissue paper dipped in water: 8 petal pieces (petal pattern 2, p179)
- Light green card stock: 3 leaves (leaf pattern 37, p175)

TECHNIQUES:

- **1:** Paper dyeing—using water
- **5:** Making centers—medium fringe center
- **4:** Petal styling—scrunching
- **8:** Attaching petals—continuous petals (create four layers working with two petal pieces at a time)
- **7:** Making leaves—card stock leaves
- **10:** Covering stems
- **12:** Attaching extra stems—single bloom
- **13:** Styling leaves and stems

Anemone

YOU WILL NEED:

- One clay bulb center on a 9in (23cm), 20-gauge (0.8mm) wire stem

- Two 4½in (11cm), 20-gauge (0.8mm) wires for leaf stems

- Light green tissue paper: one 12 x ½in (30 x 1.2cm) strip for stem, two 6 x ½in (15 x 1.2cm) strips for leaf stems

- Black tissue paper: one 2 x 2in (5 x 5cm) piece for clay center, and one 3 x 5in (7.5 x 12cm) piece for medium fringed center

- Pink, purple, or light purple tissue paper dipped in water or bleach: 9 petals (petal pattern 6, p179)

- Light green card stock: 2 leaves (leaf pattern 21, p172)

TECHNIQUES:

- **2:** Paper bleaching

- **5:** Making centers—clay centers

- **5:** Making centers—medium fringe center

- **4:** Petal styling—scrunching

- **8:** Attaching petals—single petals (arrange three petals evenly around the center, then add the remaining six petals randomly)

- **7:** Making leaves—card stock leaves

- **10:** Covering stems

- **12:** Attaching extra stems—single bloom

- **13:** Styling leaves and stems

Oriental Poppy

YOU WILL NEED:

- One clay bulb center on a 9in (23cm), 20-gauge (0.8mm) wire stem
- Two 4½in (11cm), 20-gauge (0.8mm) wires for leaf stems
- Light green tissue paper: one 2 x 2in (5 x 5cm) piece for center, one 12 x ½in (30 x 1.2cm) strip for stem, two 6 x ½in (15 x 1.2cm) strips for leaf stems
- Black tissue paper: one 3 x 5in (7.5 x 12cm) piece for medium fringed center
- Red, orange, or light orange tissue paper painted with red or orange stripes: 12 petals to create 6 double petals (petal pattern 6, p179)
- Light green card stock: 2 leaves (leaf patterns 27 and 28, p173)

TECHNIQUES:

- **3:** Paper painting—painting center accents and acrylic craft paint stripes
- **5:** Making centers— clay bulb center
- **5:** Making centers—medium fringe center
- **4:** Petal styling—scrunching
- **8:** Attaching petals—double petals (arrange the 5 double petals randomly around the center)
- **7:** Making leaves—card stock leaves
- **10:** Covering stems
- **12:** Attaching extra stems—single bloom
- **13:** Styling leaves and stems

Bouquet

PROJECT

TECHNIQUES:

• pages 158–159

Corsage, boutonnière & hairpin

PROJECT

TECHNIQUES:

• pages 160–161

Corsage A

Corsage B

Corsage C

Iceland Poppy

YOU WILL NEED:

- One clay bulb center on a 9in (23cm), 20-gauge (0.8mm) wire stem
- Two 4½in (11cm), 20-gauge (0.8mm) wires for leaf stems
- Light green tissue paper: one 2 x 2in (5 x 5cm) piece for center, one 12 x ½in (30 x 1.2cm) strip for stem, two 6 x ½in (15 x 1.2cm) strips for leaf stems
- Yellow tissue paper: one 3 x 5in (7.5 x 12cm) piece for medium fringed center
- Orange, golden yellow, light yellow, peach, or white tissue paper dipped in water: 8 petal pieces for 4 double petals (petal pattern 6, p179)
- Light green card stock: 2 leaves (leaf patterns 27 and 28, p173)

TECHNIQUES:

- **1:** Paper dyeing—using water
- **5:** Making centers— clay bulb center
- **3:** Paper painting—painting center accents
- **5:** Making centers—medium fringe center
- **4:** Petal styling—scrunching
- **8:** Attaching petals—double petals (arrange the 4 double petals evenly around the center)
- **7:** Making leaves—card stock leaves
- **10:** Covering stems
- **12:** Attaching extra stems—single bloom
- **13:** Styling leaves and stems

California Poppy

YOU WILL NEED:

- One 9in (23cm), 20-gauge (0.8mm) wire stem
- One 4½in (11cm), 20-gauge (0.8mm) wires for leaf stem
- Light green tissue paper: one 12 x ½in (30 x 1.2cm) strip for stem, one 6 x ½in (15 x 1.2cm) strip for leaf stem
- Yellow tissue paper: one 2 x 3in (5 x 7.5cm) piece for small fringed center
- Hot pink tissue paper: one 1 x 2in (2.5 x 5cm) piece for calyx
- Light orange tissue paper dipped in water: 4 petals (petal pattern 22, p183)
- Light green card stock: 1 leaf (leaf pattern 25, p173)

TECHNIQUES:

- **1:** Paper dyeing—using water
- **5:** Making centers—small fringe center
- **4:** Petal styling—scrunching
- **8:** Attaching petals—single petals
- **7:** Making leaves—card stock leaves
- **9:** Attaching the calyx (arrange the strip of tissue paper around the base of the bloom to form a complete collar)
- **10:** Covering stems
- **12:** Attaching extra stems—single bloom
- **13:** Styling leaves and stems

Godetia

YOU WILL NEED:

- Five 4½in (11cm), 20-gauge (0.8mm) wires for flower stems
- Five 4½in (11cm), 20-gauge (0.8mm) wires for leaf stems
- One 9in (23cm), 18-gauge (1mm) wire for main stem
- Green tissue paper: one 12 x ½in (30 x 1.2cm) strip for main stem, ten 6 x ½in (15 x 1.2cm) strips for smaller stems
- Yellow tissue paper: five 2 x 3in (5 x 7.5cm) pieces for small fringed centers
- Light pink tissue paper dipped in pink dye: 40 petal pieces, 4 double petals per small bloom (petal pattern 22, p183)
- Green card stock: 5 leaves (leaf pattern 35, p175)

TECHNIQUES:

- **1:** Paper dyeing—dyeing colored tissue paper
- **5:** Making centers—small fringe center
- **4:** Petal styling—scrunching
- **8:** Attaching petals—double petals (arrange four double petals evenly around each of the five fringed centers to create the small blooms)
- **7:** Making leaves—card stock leaves
- **10:** Covering stems
- **12:** Attaching extra stems—cluster (attach all five leaves directly below the cluster of blooms, joining each stem at the same height)
- **13:** Styling leaves and stems

Nasturtium

YOU WILL NEED:

- One single cotton swab center on one 9in (23cm), 22-gauge (0.65mm) wire stem
- Two 9in (23cm), 22-gauge (0.65mm) wire for leaf stems
- Light green tissue paper: three 12 x ½in (30 x 1.2cm) strips for main stem and leaf stems
- Light yellow tissue paper: one 2 x 2in (5 x 5cm) piece for cotton swab center
- Golden yellow tissue paper: 1 cuff piece for cotton swab center (cuff pattern 4, p189)
- Red, orange, golden yellow, or light yellow tissue paper dipped in bleach: 5 petal pieces (petal pattern 22, p183)
- Green and light green card stock: 2 leaves (leaf pattern 6, 169)

TECHNIQUES:

- **2:** Paper bleaching—dipped
- **5:** Making centers—cuffed single cotton swab center
- **4:** Petal styling—scrunching
- **8:** Attaching petals—single petals (arrange the petals randomly around the cuffed center)
- **7:** Making leaves—card stock leaves
- **10:** Covering stems
- **12:** Attaching extra stems—single bloom (create the stem joints 4–6in (10–15cm) below the leaves and bloom for the lengthy stems)
- **13:** Styling leaves and stems

Oleander

YOU WILL NEED:

- Three single cotton swab centers on three 4½in (11cm), 22-gauge (0.65mm) wire stems
- Five 4½in (11cm), 22-gauge (0.65mm) wire stems for buds
- Three 4½in (11cm), 22-gauge (0.65mm) wires for leaf stems
- One 9in (23cm), 18-gauge (1mm) wire for main stem
- Green tissue paper: one 12 x ½in (30 x 1.2cm) strip for main stem and eleven 6 x ½in (15 x 1.2cm) strips for small stems
- Light yellow tissue paper: three 2 x 2in (5 x 5cm) pieces for cotton swab centers and five 1 x 10in (2.5 x 25cm) strips for buds
- Yellow tissue paper: 3 cuff pieces for cotton swab centers (cuff pattern 5, p189)
- White tissue paper dipped in water: 30 petal pieces, 5 double petals per small bloom (petal pattern 22, p183)
- Green card stock: 3 leaves (leaf pattern 35, p175)

TECHNIQUES:

- **1:** Paper dyeing—using water
- **5:** Making centers—cuffed single cotton swab center
- **4:** Petal styling—scrunching
- **8:** Attaching petals—double petals (arrange 5 double petals evenly around each of the 3 cuffed centers to create the small blooms)
- **6:** Making berries and buds—rolled paper buds
- **7:** Making leaves—card stock leaves
- **10:** Covering stems
- **12:** Attaching extra stems—cluster (attach the three leaves directly below the cluster of blooms, joining each stem at the same height)
- **13:** Styling leaves and stems

Dogwood

YOU WILL NEED:

- One 24in (60cm) foraged tree branch
- Brown tissue paper: five 2 x ½in (5 x 1.2cm) strips to cover the bases of blooms
- Cream tissue paper dipped in bleach: 40 petal pieces, 4 double petals per bloom (petal pattern 23, p183)
- Light green tissue paper: five 2 x 3in (5 x 7.5cm) pieces for small fringed centers and 5 leaves (leaf patterns 38 and 39, p175)

TECHNIQUES:

- **2:** Paper bleaching—dipped
- **5:** Making centers—small fringe center
- **4:** Petal styling—pleating
- **8:** Attaching petals—double petals (arrange four double petals evenly around each fringed center)
- **7:** Making leaves—small tissue paper leaves
- **11:** Attaching leaves—tissue paper leaves
- **12:** Attaching extra stems—branch

Wild Rose

YOU WILL NEED:

- One cotton swab center on a 9in (23cm), 20-gauge (0.8mm) wire stem
- One clay bud on a 4½in (11cm), 20-gauge (0.8mm) wire stem
- Three 4½in (11cm), 20-gauge (0.8mm) wires for leaf stems
- Green tissue paper: one 12 x ½in (30 x 1.2cm) strip for main stem, four 6 x ½in (15 x 1.2cm) strips for smaller stems, two cuff pieces for bud and bloom calyx (cuff pattern 2, p189)
- Yellow tissue paper: one 2 x 2in (5 x 5cm) piece for cotton swab center and one 2 x 3in (5 x 7.5cm) piece for small fringed center
- Hot pink tissue paper dipped in bleach: one 2 x 2in (5 x 5cm) piece for bud, 10 petal pieces to create 5 double petals (petal pattern 23, p183)
- Green card stock: 3 leaves (leaf pattern 36, p175)

TECHNIQUES:

- **2:** Paper bleaching—dipped
- **5:** Making centers—single cotton swab center
- **5:** Making centers—small fringe center
- **4:** Petal styling—pleating
- **8:** Attaching petals—double petals (attach the 5 double petals evenly around the center)
- **6:** Making berries and buds—oblong clay buds
- **7:** Making leaves—card stock leaves
- **9:** Attaching the calyx
- **10:** Covering stems
- **12:** Attaching extra stems—single bloom (join 2 leaf stems and the bud stem together, then attach those joined stems to the bloom stem, then add the last leaf below the bloom)
- **13:** Styling leaves and stems

Saucer Magnolia

YOU WILL NEED:

- One clay oblong center on a 9in (23cm), 20-gauge (0.8mm) wire stem
- Two 4½in (11cm), 20-gauge (0.8mm) wires for leaf stems
- Green tissue paper: one 12 x ½in (30 x 1.2cm) strip for stem, two 6 x ½in (15 x 1.2cm) strips for leaf stems
- Light yellow tissue paper: one 2 x 2in (5 x 5cm) piece for center
- Golden yellow tissue paper: one 3 x 5in (7.5 x 12cm) piece for medium fringed center
- White tissue paper painted with pink stripes: 16 petal pieces to create 8 double petals (petal pattern 39, p186)
- Green card stock: 2 leaves (leaf pattern 8, p169)

TECHNIQUES:

- **5:** Making centers—oblong clay center
- **3:** Paper painting—acrylic craft paint stripes and alcohol-based marker (to create dotted texture on clay center)
- **5:** Making centers—medium fringe center
- **4:** Petal styling—scrunching
- **8:** Attaching petals—double petals (create four layers of 4 double petals placing the petals at random around the center)
- **4:** Petal styling—scissor curling (curl a few of the petals in various directions)
- **7:** Making leaves—card stock leaves
- **10:** Covering stems
- **12:** Attaching extra stems—single bloom
- **13:** Styling leaves and stems

Cherry Blossom Branch With Buds

YOU WILL NEED:

- One 24in (60cm) foraged tree branch
- Three clay buds without wire stems
- Brown tissue paper: eight 2 x ½in (5 x 1.2cm) strips to cover the bases of blooms and buds
- Light yellow tissue paper: five 2 x 3in (5 x 7.5cm) pieces for small fringed centers
- White tissue paper with red painted stripes: three 2 x 2in (5 x 5cm) pieces for clay buds and 25 petal pieces, 5 petals per small bloom (petal pattern 31, p185)
- Light green tissue paper: 5 leaves (leaf patterns 38 and 39, p175)

TECHNIQUES:

- **3:** Paper painting—acrylic craft paint stripes
- **5:** Making centers—small fringe center (create without wire stems)
- **4:** Petal styling—cupping
- **8:** Attaching petals—single petals (place five petals randomly around each of the five fringe centers)
- **6:** Making berries and buds—round clay buds
- **7:** Making leaves—small tissue paper leaves
- **11:** Attaching leaves—tissue paper leaves
- **12:** Attaching extra stems—branch

Petite Camellia

YOU WILL NEED:

- Two 9in (23cm), 20-gauge (0.8mm) wire stems
- One clay bud on a 4½in (11cm), 22-gauge (0.65mm) wire stem
- Three 4½in (11cm), 22-gauge (0.65mm) wires for leaf stems
- Green tissue paper: two 12 x ½in (30 x 1.2cm) strips for main stems, four 6 x ½in (15 x 1.2cm) strips for small stems
- Light yellow tissue paper: two 2 x 3in (5 x 7.5cm) pieces for small fringed centers
- Light pink tissue paper: one 2 x 2in (5 x 5cm) piece for clay bud
- Light pink tissue paper dipped in bleach: 32 petal pieces, 8 double petals for each small bloom (petal pattern 31, p185)
- Green card stock: 3 leaves (leaf pattern 37, p175)

TECHNIQUES:

- **2:** Paper bleaching—dipped
- **5:** Making centers—small fringe center
- **4:** Petal styling—cupping
- **8:** Attaching petals—double petals (arrange 8 double petals per small bloom, working in two layers of four petals each and attaching the petals evenly around the fringed centers)
- **6:** Making berries and buds—round clay buds
- **7:** Making leaves—card stock leaves
- **10:** Covering stems
- **12:** Attaching extra stems—cluster
- **13:** Styling leaves and stems

Indian Paintbrush

YOU WILL NEED:

- Six burgundy single pip stamens on six 4½in (11cm), 22-gauge (0.65mm) wire stems
- Five 4½in (11cm), 22-gauge (0.65mm) wire stems for buds
- Three 4½in (11cm), 22-gauge (0.65mm) wires for leaf stems
- One 9in (23cm), 18-gauge (1mm) wire for main stem
- Light green tissue paper: one 20 x ½in (50 x 1.2cm) strip for main stem, fourteen 6 x ½in (15 x 1.2cm) strips for small stems
- Red tissue paper: five 1 x 10in (2.5 x 25cm) strips for buds, 10 petal pieces, create 4 blooms with 2 petal pieces each and 2 blooms with 1 petal piece each (petal pattern 10, p180)
- Light green card stock: 3 leaves (leaf patterns 22 and 23, p172)

TECHNIQUES:

- **5:** Making centers—single pip stamen
- **4:** Petal styling—scrunching
- **8:** Attaching petals—continuous petals (for each small bloom attach one petal piece evenly around the stamen center, for the 4 larger blooms arrange another petal piece, lining up the second layer of petals behind the petals of the first layer)
- **4:** Petal styling—scissor curling (curl all petals, allowing the outer petals to curl more tightly than the inner petals)
- **6:** Making berries and buds—rolled paper buds
- **7:** Making leaves—card stock leaves
- **10:** Covering stems
- **12:** Attaching extra stems—spike (begin with a larger bloom and attach it to the end of the main stem, then arrange the other 3 larger blooms along the main stem, followed by the 2 smaller blooms and the 5 buds below the blooms, and attach the 3 leaves after the final bud)
- **13:** Styling leaves and stems

Flame Vine

YOU WILL NEED:

- Six yellow single pip stamens on six 4½in (11cm), 22-gauge (0.65mm) wire stems
- Three 4½in (11cm), 22-gauge (0.65mm) wire stems for buds
- Two 18in (46cm), 18-gauge (1mm) wires taped together for main stem
- Orange tissue paper: three 1 x 10in (2.5 x 25cm) strips for buds, 12 petal pieces, 2 pieces per small bloom (petal pattern 10, p180)
- Green tissue paper: one 20 x ½in (50 x 1.2cm) strip for main stem, nine 6 x ½in (15 x 1.2cm) strips for small stems, 6 leaves (leaf patterns 38 and 39, p175)

TECHNIQUES:

- **5:** Making centers—single pip stamen
- **4:** Petal styling—scrunching
- **8:** Attaching petals—continuous petals (for each small bloom attach one petal piece evenly around the stamen center, then arrange a second petal piece, lining up the petals behind the petals of the first layer)
- **4:** Petal styling—scissor curling (curl all petals, allowing the outer petals to curl more tightly than the inner petals)
- **6:** Making berries and buds—rolled paper buds
- **7:** Making leaves—small tissue paper leaves
- **10:** Covering stems
- **11:** Attaching leaves—tissue paper leaves
- **12:** Attaching extra stems—vine (attach the blooms and buds in random order at the top end of the main stem; join each stem close together to get a clustered appearance)
- **13:** Styling leaves and stems

Honeysuckle

YOU WILL NEED:

- Five yellow single pip stamens on five 4½in (11cm), 22-gauge (0.65mm) wire stems
- Three 4½in (11cm), 22-gauge (0.65mm) wire stems for buds
- Two 18in (46cm), 18-gauge (1mm) wires taped together for main stem
- White tissue paper: three 1 x 10in (2.5 x 25cm) strips for buds, 5 petal pieces, 1 piece per small bloom (petal pattern 10, p180)
- Peach tissue paper: 5 petal pieces, pair with 5 white petal pieces before assembling (petal pattern 10, p180)
- Light green tissue paper: one 20 x ½in (50 x 1.2cm) strip for main stem, eight 6 x ½in (15 x 1.2cm) strips for small stems, 6 small leaves and 2 large leaves (leaf patterns 38 and 39, p175)

TECHNIQUES:

- **5:** Making centers—single pip stamen
- **4:** Petal styling—scrunching
- **8:** Attaching petals—continuous petals (for each small bloom attach 1 white petal piece evenly around the stamen center, then arrange 1 peach petal piece, lining up the second layer of petals behind the petals of the first layer)
- **4:** Petal styling—scissor curling (curl all petals, allowing the outer petals to curl more tightly than the inner petals)
- **6:** Making berries and buds—rolled paper buds
- **7:** Making leaves—small tissue paper leaves
- **10:** Covering stems
- **11:** Attaching leaves—tissue paper leaves
- **12:** Attaching extra stems—vine (begin with attaching two leaf pieces to the end of the main stem, add one bloom and one bud approximately 3in (7.5cm) down the stem, then add two leaf pieces at the joint; repeat creating two more groupings of two blooms, one bud and two leaf pieces)
- **13:** Styling leaves and stems

Oxalis

YOU WILL NEED:

- Three 6in (15cm), 20-gauge (0.8mm) wire stems
- Burgundy tissue paper: three 8 x ½in (20 x 1.2cm) strips for stems
- Dark plum card stock: 3 leaves (leaf pattern 3, p168)

TECHNIQUES:

- **7**: Making leaves—card stock leaves
- **10**: Covering stems
- **12**: Attaching extra stems—cluster (join the 3 stems directly below the leaf and bend the leaves approximately 80–90° away from the center joint)
- **13**: Styling leaves and stems

Sweet Potato Vine

YOU WILL NEED:

- Five 4½in (11cm), 22-gauge (0.65mm) wires for leaf stems
- Two 18in (46cm), 18-gauge (1mm) wires taped together for main stem
- Burgundy tissue paper: one 20 x ½in (50 x 1.2cm) strip for main stem, five 6 x ½in (15 x 1.2cm) strips for leaf stems
- Burgundy card stock: 5 leaves—2 small, 2 medium, and 1 large (leaf patterns 10, 11, and 12, p170)

TECHNIQUES:

- **7:** Making leaves—card stock leaves
- **10:** Covering stems
- **12:** Attaching extra stems—vine (attach a small leaf at the end of the main stem, then a medium leaf, followed by a large leaf, then the other medium leaf and finally the other small leaf)
- **13:** Styling leaves and stems

Berry Stem

YOU WILL NEED:

- Six or eight clay berries on six or eight 4½in (11cm), 20-gauge (0.8mm) wire stems
- One 18in (46cm), 18-gauge (1mm) wire for main stem
- Red tissue paper: six or eight 2 x 2in (5 x 5cm) pieces for clay berries
- Brown tissue paper: one 12 x ½in (30 x 1.2cm) strip for main stem, six or eight 6 x ½in (15 x 1.2cm) strips for small stems

TECHNIQUES:

- **6:** Making berries and buds—round clay berries
- **10:** Covering stems
- **12:** Attaching extra stems—spike
- **13:** Styling leaves and stems

Pokeweed

YOU WILL NEED:

- Ten clay berries on ten 4½in (11cm), 22-gauge (0.65mm) wire stems
- Three 4½in (11cm), 22-gauge (0.65mm) wires for leaf stems
- One 18in (46cm), 18-gauge (1mm) wire for main stem
- Fuchsia tissue paper: one 20 x ½in (50 x 1.2cm) strip for main stem, thirteen 6 x ½in (15 x 1.2cm) strips for small stems
- Purple tissue paper: ten 2 x 2in (5 x 5cm) pieces for berries
- Light green card stock: 3 leaves (leaf pattern 8, p169)

TECHNIQUES:

- **6:** Making berries and buds—round clay berries
- **7:** Making leaves—card stock leaves
- **10:** Covering stems
- **12:** Attaching extra stems—spike (attach one berry to the end of the main stem and attach the remaining berries approximately ¼–½in (0.6–1.2cm) apart along the main stem)
- **13:** Styling leaves and stems

Wheat

YOU WILL NEED:

- One 15in (38cm), 20-gauge (0.8mm) wire stem
- Light green tissue paper: one 15 x ½in (38 x 1.2cm) strip for stem
- White tissue paper dyed light green: two 2 x 5in (5 x 12cm) pieces for bottlebrush center
- Light green card stock: 1 leaf piece cut lengthwise down the center to create 2 thin leaves (leaf pattern 14, p170)

TECHNIQUES:

- **5:** Making centers—bottlebrush center
- **7:** Making leaves—card stock leaves
- **10:** Covering stems
- **11:** Attaching leaves—card stock leaves
- **12:** Attaching extra stems—single bloom
- **13:** Styling leaves and stems

Lavender

YOU WILL NEED:

- One 12in (30cm), 20-gauge (0.8mm) wire stem
- Sage green tissue paper: one 15 x ½in (38 x 1.2cm) strip for stem
- Light purple tissue paper: two 2 x 5in (5 x 12cm) pieces for bottlebrush center

TECHNIQUES:

- **5:** Making centers—bottlebrush center
- **10:** Covering stems
- **13:** Styling leaves and stems

Caladium

YOU WILL NEED:

- One 12in (30cm), 20-gauge (0.8mm) wire stem
- Green tissue paper: one 15 x ½in (38 x 1.2cm) strip for stem
- Green card stock: 1 leaf (leaf pattern 18, p172)

TECHNIQUES:

- **3:** Paper painting—painting card stock leaves
- **7:** Making leaves—card stock leaves
- **10:** Covering stems
- **13:** Styling leaves and stems

Pink Cordyline

YOU WILL NEED:

- One 15in (38cm), 18-gauge (1mm) wire stem
- Burgundy tissue paper: one 20 x ½in (50 x 1.2cm) strip for stem
- Burgundy card stock: 1 leaf (leaf pattern 16, p171)

TECHNIQUES:

- **3:** Paper painting—painting card stock leaves
- **7:** Making leaves—card stock leaves
- **10:** Covering stems
- **13:** Styling leaves and stems

Philodendron

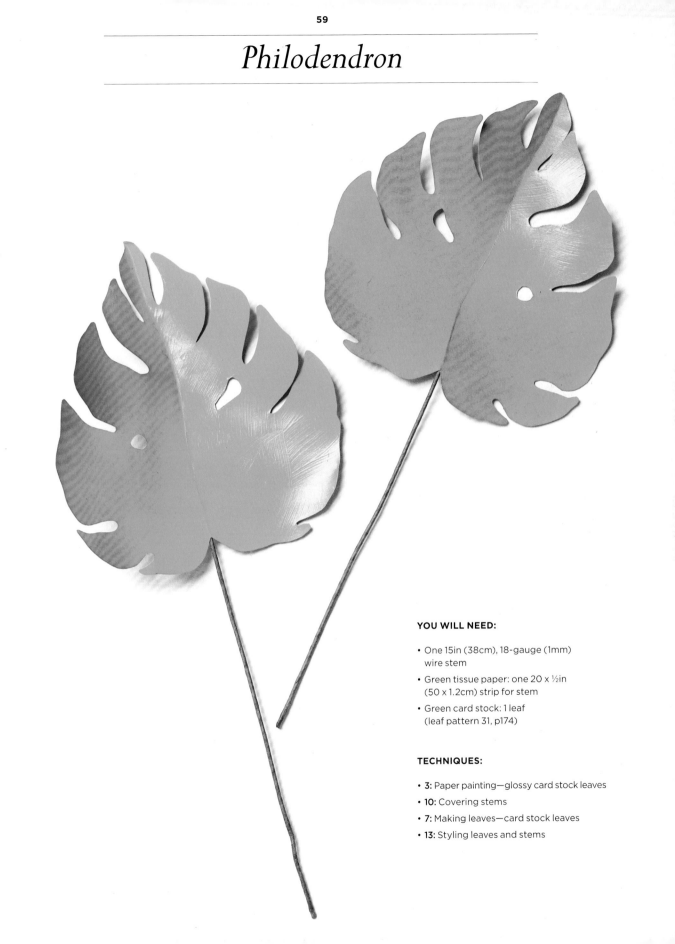

YOU WILL NEED:

- One 15in (38cm), 18-gauge (1mm) wire stem
- Green tissue paper: one 20 x ½in (50 x 1.2cm) strip for stem
- Green card stock: 1 leaf (leaf pattern 31, p174)

TECHNIQUES:

- **3:** Paper painting—glossy card stock leaves
- **10:** Covering stems
- **7:** Making leaves—card stock leaves
- **13:** Styling leaves and stems

Croton

YOU WILL NEED:

- One 12in (30cm), 20-gauge (0.8mm) wire stem
- Red tissue paper: one 15 x ½in (38 x 1.2cm) strip for stem
- Red card stock: 1 leaf (leaf pattern 2, p168)

TECHNIQUES:

- **3:** Paper painting—painting card stock leaves
- **7:** Making leaves—card stock leaves
- **10:** Covering stems
- **13:** Styling leaves and stems

Begonia "Escargot"

YOU WILL NEED:

- One 12in (30cm), 20-gauge (0.8mm) wire stem
- Dark green tissue paper: one 15 x ½in (38 x 1.2cm) strip for stem
- Dark green card stock: 1 leaf (leaf pattern 48, p178)

TECHNIQUES:

- **3:** Paper painting—painting card stock leaves
- **7:** Making leaves—card stock leaves
- **10:** Covering stems
- **13:** Styling leaves and stems

Garden Rose

YOU WILL NEED:

- One 9in (23cm), 20-gauge (0.8mm) wire stem
- Two 4½in (11cm), 20-gauge (0.8mm) wires for leaf stems
- Green tissue paper: one 12 x ½in (30 x 1.2cm) strip for stem, two 6 x ½in (15 x 1.2cm) strips for leaf stems, 1 calyx piece (cuff pattern 1, p189)
- Yellow tissue paper: one 3 x 5in (7.5 x 12cm) piece for medium fringed center
- Light yellow or blush tissue paper dipped in bleach or light yellow tissue paper with pale pink painted stripes: 8 small petal pieces and 8–12 large petal pieces (petal patterns 3 and 4, p179)
- Green card stock: 2 leaves (leaf pattern 36, p175)

TECHNIQUES:

- **2:** Paper bleaching—dipped (for the light yellow and blush roses)
- **3:** Paper painting—acrylic craft paint stripes (for the yellow rose with pink stripes)
- **5:** Making centers—medium fringe center
- **4:** Petal styling—scissor curling tops of all petals (curl the petals before assembling the bloom)
- **4:** Petal styling—pleating and scrunching (pleat the petals first, then scrunch)
- **8:** Attaching petals—single petals (first arrange the eight small petals randomly around the center, then arrange the 8–12 large petals randomly around the bloom)
- **9:** Attaching the calyx
- **7:** Making leaves—card stock leaves
- **10:** Covering stems
- **12:** Attaching extra stems—single bloom
- **13:** Styling leaves and stems

Juliet Rose

YOU WILL NEED:

- One 9in (23cm), 20-gauge (0.8mm) wire stem
- One 4½in (11cm), 20-gauge (0.8mm) wire for leaf stem
- Light green tissue paper: one 12 x ½in (30 x 1.2cm) strip for stem, one 6 x ½in (15 x 1.2cm) strip for leaf stem, 1 calyx piece (cuff pattern 1, p189)
- Light orange tissue paper: one 3 x 5in (7.5 x 12cm) piece for medium fringed center
- Light pink tissue paper dipped in darker pink dye: 10 small petal pieces, 15 medium petal pieces, and 6 large petal pieces (petal patterns 5, 7, and 8, p179)
- Light green card stock: 1 leaf (leaf pattern 36, p175)

TECHNIQUES:

- **1:** Paper dyeing—dyeing colored tissue paper
- **5:** Making centers—medium fringe center
- **4:** Petal styling—scrunching for all petals and pleating for the 6 large petals
- **8:** Attaching petals—double petals (begin with the 5 small double petals and then add the 5 medium double petals; make sure you attach each double petal in a clockwise sequence around the bloom)
- **8:** Attaching petals—single petals (after attaching the small and medium double petals, arrange the 5 medium single petals spaced randomly around the bloom, followed by the 5 large petals)
- **9:** Attaching the calyx
- **7:** Making leaves—card stock leaves
- **10:** Covering stems
- **12:** Attaching extra stems—single bloom
- **13:** Styling leaves and stems

Zinnia

YOU WILL NEED:

- One clay oblong center on a 9in (23cm), 20-gauge (0.8mm) wire stem
- Four 4½in (11cm), 22-gauge (0.65mm) wires for leaf stems
- Green tissue paper: one 12 x ½in (30 x 1.2cm) strip for stem, four 6 x ½in (15 x 1.2cm) strips for leaf stems
- Burgundy tissue paper: one 2 x 2in (5 x 5cm) piece for clay center
- Golden yellow tissue paper: one 2 x 3in (5 x 7.5cm) piece for small fringed center
- Orange tissue paper: 6 petal pieces (petal pattern 45, p187)
- Green card stock: 4 leaves (leaf pattern 37, p175)

TECHNIQUES:

- **5:** Making centers—oblong clay center
- **5:** Making centers—small fringe center (apply the fringe approximately halfway up the clay center)
- **4:** Petal styling—scrunching
- **8:** Attaching petals—continuous petals (create three layers of two petal pieces, placing the petals evenly around the center and filling in empty spaces between previously placed petals)
- **7:** Making leaves—card stock leaves
- **10:** Covering stems
- **12:** Attaching extra stems—single bloom (arrange the leaves in pairs along the length below the bloom)
- **13:** Styling leaves and stems

Coneflower

YOU WILL NEED:

- One clay oblong center on a 9in (23cm), 18-gauge (1mm) wire stem
- Three 4½in (11cm), 20-gauge (0.8mm) wires for leaf stems
- Light green tissue paper: one 12 x ½in (30 x 1.2cm) strip for stem, three 6 x ½in (15 x 1.2cm) strips for leaf stems
- Orange tissue paper: one 2 x 2in (5 x 5cm) piece for clay center
- Fuchsia tissue paper: 6 petal pieces (petal pattern 46, p187)
- Light green card stock: 3 leaves (leaf patterns 22 and 23, p172)

TECHNIQUES:

- **5:** Making centers—oblong clay center
- **3:** Paper painting—alcohol-based marker (create orange dots on top of the orange tissue paper center)
- **4:** Petal styling—scrunching
- **8:** Attaching petals—continuous petals (attach petals around the bottom of the clay center rather than directly to the wire stem; arrange three petal pieces evenly around the center, then add the last three petal pieces in a second layer)
- **4:** Petal styling—scissor curling (curl all of the petals downward)
- **7:** Making leaves—card stock leaves
- **10:** Covering stems
- **12:** Attaching extra stems—single bloom
- **13:** Styling leaves and stems

Black-Eyed Susan

YOU WILL NEED:

- One clay oblong center on a 9in (23cm), 18-gauge (1mm) wire stem
- Two 4½in (11cm), 20-gauge (0.8mm) wires for leaf stems
- Green tissue paper: one 12 x ½in (30 x 1.2cm) strip for stem, two 6 x ½in (15 x 1.2cm) strips for leaf stems
- Brown tissue paper: one 2 x 2in (5 x 5cm) piece for clay center
- Golden yellow tissue paper: 6 petal pieces (petal pattern 46, p187)
- Green card stock: 2 leaves (leaf patterns 22 and 23, p172)

TECHNIQUES:

- **5:** Making centers—oblong clay center
- **4:** Petal styling—scrunching
- **8:** Attaching petals—continuous petals (attach petals around the bottom of the clay center rather than directly to the wire stem; arrange three petal pieces evenly around the center, then add the last three petal pieces in a second layer)
- **4:** Petal styling—scissor curling (only curl a few petals for a natural look)
- **7:** Making leaves—card stock leaves
- **10:** Covering stems
- **12:** Attaching extra stems—single bloom
- **13:** Styling leaves and stems

Shasta Daisy

YOU WILL NEED:

- One clay bulb center on a 9in (23cm), 20-gauge (0.8mm) wire stem
- One clay bud on a 9in (23cm), 20-gauge (0.8mm) wire stem
- Two 4½in (11cm), 20-gauge (0.8mm) wires for leaf stems
- Green tissue paper: one 2 x 12 x ½in (30 x 1.2cm) strip for stems, two 6 x ½in (15 x 1.2cm) strips for leaf stems
- Golden yellow tissue paper: one 2 x 2in (5 x 5cm) piece for center
- White tissue paper dipped in water: one 2 x 2in (5 x 5cm) piece for bud, 4 petal pieces (petal pattern 46, p187)
- Green card stock: 2 leaves (leaf pattern 25, p173)

TECHNIQUES:

- **1:** Paper dyeing—using water
- **5:** Making centers— clay bulb center
- **4:** Petal styling—scrunching
- **8:** Attaching petals—continuous petals (arrange the first two petal pieces evenly around the clay center, then add the next two pieces evenly, filling in empty spaces around the center)
- **6:** Making berries and buds—round clay bud
- **7:** Making leaves—card stock leaves
- **10:** Covering stems
- **12:** Attaching extra stems—single bloom
- **13:** Styling leaves and stems

African Daisy

YOU WILL NEED:

- One clay bulb center on a 9in (23cm), 20-gauge (0.8mm) wire stem
- One 4½in (11cm), 20-gauge (0.8mm) wire for leaf stem
- Green tissue paper: one 12 x ½in (30 x 1.2cm) strip for stem, one 6 x ½in (15 x 1.2cm) strip for leaf stem
- Dark blue or purple tissue paper: one 2 x 2in (5 x 5cm) piece for clay center
- Light purple tissue paper: 2 petal pieces (petal pattern 45, p187)
- Green card stock: 1 leaf (leaf pattern 46, p176)

TECHNIQUES:

- **5:** Making centers—clay centers
- **4:** Petal styling—scrunching
- **8:** Attaching petals—continuous petals (arrange the first petal piece evenly around the clay center, then add the second piece evenly, filling in empty spaces around the center)
- **7:** Making leaves—card stock leaves
- **10:** Covering stems
- **12:** Attaching extra stems—single bloom
- **13:** Styling leaves and stems

Blue Aster

YOU WILL NEED:

- Eight 4½in (11cm), 22-gauge (0.65mm) wire stems (5 stems for small blooms and 3 stems for leaves)
- One 9in (23cm), 18-gauge (1mm) wire for main stem
- Green tissue paper: one 12 x ½in (30 x 1.2cm) strip for main stem, eight 6 x ½in (15 x 1.2cm) strips for small stems
- Light yellow tissue paper: five 2 x 3in (5 x 7.5cm) pieces for small fringed centers
- Blue tissue paper with bleached stripes: 10 petal pieces, 2 petal pieces per small bloom (petal pattern 44, p187)
- Green card stock: 3 leaves (leaf patterns 22 and 23, p172)

TECHNIQUES:

- **2:** Paper bleaching—stripes
- **5:** Making centers—small fringe center
- **4:** Petal styling—scrunching
- **8:** Attaching petals—continuous petals (arrange two petal pieces evenly around each fringed center)
- **7:** Making leaves—card stock leaves
- **10:** Covering stems
- **12:** Attaching extra stems—spike
- **13:** Styling leaves and stems

Cosmos

YOU WILL NEED:

- One 12in (30cm), 20-gauge (0.8mm) wire stem
- One 4½in (11cm), 20-gauge (0.8mm) wire for leaf stem
- Light green tissue paper: one 15 x ½in (38 x 1.2cm) strip for stem, one 6 x ½in (15 x 1.2cm) strip for leaf stem
- Golden yellow tissue paper: one 2 x 3in (5 x 7.5cm) piece for small fringed center
- Fuchsia tissue paper with hot pink painted stripes: 8 petal pieces (petal pattern 42, p187)
- Light green card stock: 1 leaf (leaf pattern 25, p173)

TECHNIQUES:

- **3:** Paper painting—acrylic craft paint stripes
- **5:** Making centers—small fringe center
- **4:** Petal styling—scrunching
- **8:** Attaching petals—continuous petals (cut the petals as one continuous piece, then divide in half, working with four petals at a time and placing them evenly around the fringe center)
- **7:** Making leaves—card stock leaves
- **10:** Covering stems
- **12:** Attaching extra stems—single bloom
- **13:** Styling leaves and stems

Chocolate Cosmos

YOU WILL NEED:

- One 12in (30cm), 20-gauge (0.8mm) wire stem
- Two 4½in (11cm), 20-gauge (0.8mm) wires for leaf stems
- Light green tissue paper: one 15 x ½in (38 x 1.2cm) strip for stem, two 6 x ½in (15 x 1.2cm) strips for leaf stem
- Brown tissue paper: one 2 x 3in (5 x 7.5cm) piece for small fringed center
- Burgundy tissue paper: 8 petal pieces (petal pattern 43, p187)
- Light green card stock: 2 leaves (leaf patterns 22 and 23, p172)

TECHNIQUES:

- **5:** Making centers—small fringe center
- **4:** Petal styling—scrunching
- **8:** Attaching petals—continuous petals (cut the petals as one continuous piece, then divide in half, working with four petals at a time and placing them evenly around the fringe center)
- **7:** Making leaves—card stock leaves
- **10:** Covering stems
- **12:** Attaching extra stems—single bloom
- **13:** Styling leaves and stems

Freesia

YOU WILL NEED:

- Three yellow single pip stamens on three 4½in (11cm), 22-gauge (0.65mm) wire stems
- Two 4½in (11cm), 22-gauge (0.65mm) wire stems for buds
- One 12in (30cm), 18-gauge (1mm) wire for main stem
- Green tissue paper: one 15 x ½in (38 x 1.2cm) strip for main stem, five 6 x ½in (15 x 1.2cm) strips for small stems
- Light orange tissue paper with bleached stripes: 4 petal pieces cut in half, 2 halves per small bloom and one piece split between 2 buds (petal pattern 30, p185)
- Green card stock: 2 leaves (leaf pattern 14, p170)

TECHNIQUES:

- **2:** Paper bleaching—stripes
- **5:** Making centers—single pip stamen
- **8:** Attaching petals—bell petals (to create these bell flowers with two layers of petals, it is easiest to tack the two petal pieces together with a small line of glue at the bottom of the petals before creating the bell shape)
- **4:** Petal styling—rolled curling for petal tips
- **6:** Making berries and buds—petaled buds
- **7:** Making leaves—card stock leaves
- **10:** Covering stems
- **11:** Attaching leaves—card stock leaves
- **12:** Attaching extra stems—spike (arrange the two petaled buds at the top of the spike, then add the three blooms)
- **13:** Styling leaves and stems

Tuberose

YOU WILL NEED:

- Six light yellow single pip stamens on six 4½in (11cm), 22-gauge (0.65mm) wire stems
- One 12in (30cm), 18-gauge (1mm) wire for main stem
- Light green tissue paper: one 15 x ½in (38 x 1.2cm) strip for main stem, six 6 x ½in (15 x 1.2cm) strips for small stems
- Cream tissue paper: 9 petal pieces, create 3 larger blooms with 2 pieces each and 3 smaller blooms with 1 piece each (petal pattern 30, p185)
- Light green card stock: 2 leaves (leaf pattern 14, p170)

TECHNIQUES:

- **5:** Making centers—single pip stamen
- **4:** Petal styling—scrunching
- **8:** Attaching petals—continuous petals (arrange one petal piece evenly around each stamen center, then for the larger blooms add a second petal piece evenly behind the first petals of three blooms)
- **7:** Making leaves—card stock leaves
- **10:** Covering stems
- **11:** Attaching leaves—card stock leaves
- **12:** Attaching extra stems—spike (arrange the three smaller blooms at the top of the spike, then add the three larger blooms below)
- **13:** Styling leaves and stems

Turquoise Ixia

YOU WILL NEED:

- Six gray single pip stamens on six 4½in (11cm), 22-gauge (0.65mm) wire stems
- One 12in (30cm), 18-gauge (1mm) wire for main stem
- Light green tissue paper: one 15 x ½in (38 x 1.2cm) strip for main stem, six 6 x ½in (15 x 1.2cm) strips for small stems
- Brown tissue paper with bleached stripes: 6 petal pieces, 1 piece per small bloom (petal pattern 30, p185)
- Green card stock: 2 leaves (leaf pattern 14, p170)

TECHNIQUES:

- **2:** Paper bleaching—stripes
- **5:** Making centers—single pip stamen
- **4:** Petal styling—scrunching
- **8:** Attaching petals—continuous petals
- **7:** Making leaves—card stock leaves
- **10:** Covering stems
- **11:** Attaching leaves—card stock leaves
- **12:** Attaching extra stems—spike (attach the blooms down the main stem in a straight row)
- **13:** Styling leaves and stems

Clematis

YOU WILL NEED:

- Four 4½in (11cm), 20-gauge (0.8mm) wire stems (1 stem for the bloom and 3 stems for the leaves)
- Two 18in (46cm), 18-gauge (1mm) wires taped together for main stem
- Light green tissue paper: one 20 x ½in (50 x 1.2cm) strip for main stem, four 6 x ½in (15 x 1.2cm) strips for small stems
- Light yellow tissue paper: one 3 x 10in (7.5 x 25cm) piece for large fringed center
- Purple tissue paper dipped in water: 16 petal pieces, 2 pieces per petal (petal pattern 37, p186)
- Light green card stock: 3 leaves (leaf patterns 10, 11, and 12, p170)

TECHNIQUES:

- **1:** Paper dyeing—using water
- **5:** Making centers—large fringe center
- **4:** Petal styling— pleating and scrunching (pleat the petals first, then scrunch to form the petals around the center)
- **8:** Attaching petals—double petals (place four double petals for the first layer evenly around the center, then fill in spaces with the last four double petals)
- **7:** Making leaves—card stock leaves
- **10:** Covering stems
- **12:** Attaching extra stems—vine (start with a small leaf at the top of the vine, the add another leaf before adding the bloom approximately 9in (23cm) from the top of the main stem)
- **13:** Styling leaves and stems

Water Lily

YOU WILL NEED:

- One clay bulb center on a 9in (23cm), 18-gauge (1mm) wire stem
- Light green tissue paper: one 12 x ½in (30 x 1.2cm) strip for stem
- Light yellow tissue paper: one 3 x 3in (7.5 x 7.5cm) piece for clay center
- Golden yellow tissue paper: one 3 x 5in (7.5 x 12cm) piece for medium fringed center
- White tissue paper dipped in yellow, peach, and pink dye: 48 petal pieces to create 24 double petals, 8 yellow, 8 peach, and 8 pink double petals (petal pattern 37, p186)
- Light green card stock: 1 leaf (leaf pattern 47, p177)

TECHNIQUES:

- **1:** Paper dyeing—dyeing white tissue paper
- **5:** Making centers— clay bulb center
- **3:** Paper painting—alcohol-based marker (to create accent clay center markings)
- **5:** Making centers—medium fringe center
- **4:** Petal styling—scrunching and pleating for all petals
- **8:** Attaching petals—double petals (working with 4 double petals at a time per layer, arrange all of the petals evenly and symmetrically around the center, for the ombré effect attach the yellow petals, then the peach, then the pink)
- **7:** Making leaves—card stock leaves
- **4:** Petal styling—pinching (use for adding lily pad leaf, pinch the card stock around the base of the bloom)
- **10:** Covering stems
- **11:** Attaching leaves—card stock leaves
- **12:** Attaching extra stems—single bloom
- **13:** Styling leaves and stems

Trillium

YOU WILL NEED:

- One 9in (23cm), 20-gauge (0.8mm) wire stem
- Three 4½in (11cm), 20-gauge (0.8mm) wires for leaf stems
- Green tissue paper: one 12 x ½in (30 x 1.2cm) strip for main stem, three 6 x ½in (15 x 1.2cm) strips for leaf stems, 6 petal pieces to create 3 double petals (petal pattern 36, p186)
- Light yellow tissue paper: one 2 x 3in (5 x 7.5cm) piece for small fringed center
- White tissue paper: 6 petal pieces to create 3 double petals (petal pattern 36, p186)
- Green card stock: 3 leaves (leaf pattern 43, p176)

TECHNIQUES:

- **5:** Making centers—small fringe center
- **4:** Petal styling—pleating
- **8:** Attaching petals—double petals (begin by arranging the three white petals evenly around the fringe center, then add the green petal, filling in the spaces between the white petals)
- **7:** Making leaves—card stock leaves
- **10:** Covering stems
- **12:** Attaching extra stems—single bloom (center each leaf below a white petal, joining each stem at the same height along the main stem)
- **13:** Styling leaves and stems

Bougainvillea

YOU WILL NEED:

- Three pink triple pip stamens on three 4½in (11cm), 20-gauge (0.8mm) wire stems
- Nine 4½in (11cm), 32-gauge (0.2mm) wire stems for petals, 3 wired petals per small bloom
- Three 4½in (11cm), 20-gauge (0.8mm) wire for leaf stems
- One 9in (23cm), 18-gauge (1mm) wire for main stem
- Green tissue paper: one 12 x ½in (30 x 1.2cm) strip for main stem, twelve 6 x ½in (15 x 1.2cm) strips for attaching small stems
- Hot pink tissue paper: 18 petals, 2 pieces per wired petal (leaf pattern 37, p175)
- Green card stock: 3 leaves (leaf pattern 37, p175)

TECHNIQUES:

- **5:** Making centers—multiple pip stamen
- **8:** Attaching petals—wired petals (arrange three petals evenly around each center)
- **4:** Petal styling—rolled curling for the petal wires
- **10:** Covering stems
- **7:** Making leaves—card stock leaves
- **12:** Attaching extra stems—cluster
- **13:** Styling leaves and stems

Day Lily

YOU WILL NEED:

- One yellow 6-pip stamen on a 12in (30cm), 18-gauge (1mm) wire stem
- Six 12in (30cm), 32-gauge (0.2mm) wire stems for petals
- Light green tissue paper: one 15 x ½in (38 x 1.2cm) strip for main stem, six 6 x ½in (15 x 1.2cm) strips for attaching petal stems
- Golden yellow tissue paper: 12 petals, 2 pieces per wired petal (petal pattern 38, p186)
- Light green card stock: 2 leaves (leaf pattern 14, p170)

TECHNIQUES:

- 5: Making centers—multiple pip stamen
- 4: Petal styling—scrunching
- 8: Attaching petals—wired petals (arrange the first three petals evenly around the stamen center, then add the last three, petals, filling in the empty spaces around the first petals)
- 4: Petal styling—rolled curling for petal wires
- 7: Making leaves—card stock leaves
- 10: Covering stems
- 11: Attaching leaves—card stock leaves
- 12: Attaching extra stems—single bloom
- 13: Styling leaves and stems

Tiger Lily

YOU WILL NEED:

- Two burgundy 6-pip stamens on two 12in (30cm), 18-gauge (1mm) wire stems
- One 12in (30cm), 18-gauge (1mm) wire stem for bud
- Fifteen 12in (30cm), 32-gauge (0.2mm) wire stems for petals
- Six 4½in (11cm), 20-gauge (0.8mm) wires for leaf stems
- Green tissue paper: three 15 x ½in (38 x 1.2cm) strips for main stems, twenty-one 6 x ½in (15 x 1.2cm) strips for attaching petals and leaf stems
- Orange tissue paper with burgundy speckling: 30 petals, 2 pieces per wired petal to create 2 blooms with 6 petals and 1 bud with 3 petals (petal pattern 38, 186)
- Green card stock: 6 leaves (leaf pattern 35, p175)

TECHNIQUES:

- **5:** Making centers—multiple pip stamen
- **3:** Paper painting—alcohol-based marker (to create the dots on petals)
- **4:** Petal styling—scrunching
- **8:** Attaching petals—wired petals (arrange the first three petals evenly around the stamen center, then add the last three petals, filling in the spaces around the first petals)
- **4:** Petal styling—rolled curling for petal wires
- **7:** Making leaves—card stock leaves
- **10:** Covering stems
- **12:** Attaching extra stems—cluster (arrange the leaves in pairs along the length below the cluster of blooms and bud, making sure to join the leaf pairs at alternating directions)
- **13:** Styling leaves and stems

Stargazer Lily

YOU WILL NEED:

- One burgundy 6-pip stamen on a 12in (30cm), 18-gauge (1mm) wire stem
- Six 12in (30cm), 32-gauge (0.2mm) wire stems for petals
- Six 4½in (11cm), 20-gauge (0.8mm) wires for leaf stems
- Green tissue paper: one 15 x ½in (38 x 1.2cm) strip for main stem, twelve 6 x ½in (15 x 1.2cm) strips for attaching petals and leaf stems
- White tissue paper painted pink with burgundy speckles: 12 petals, 2 pieces per wired petal (petal pattern 38, p186)
- Green card stock: 6 leaves (leaf pattern 35, p175)

TECHNIQUES:

- **5:** Making centers—multiple pip stamen
- **3:** Paper painting—painting individual petals and using alcohol-based marker (to create dots on petals)
- **4:** Petal styling—scrunching
- **8:** Attaching petals—wired petals (arrange the first three petals evenly around the stamen center, then add the last three petals, filling in the empty spaces around the first petals)
- **4:** Petal styling—rolled curling for petal wires
- **7:** Making leaves—card stock leaves
- **10:** Covering stems
- **12:** Attaching extra stems—single bloom (arrange the leaves in pairs along the length, making sure to join the leaf pairs at alternating directions)
- **13:** Styling leaves and stems

Delphinium

YOU WILL NEED:

- Six black single pip stamens on six 4½in (11cm), 22-gauge (0.65mm) wire stems
- Two 4½in (11cm), 22-gauge (0.65mm) wires for leaf stems
- One 18in (46cm), 18-gauge (1mm) wire for main stem
- Light green tissue paper: one 20 x ½in (50 x 1.2cm) strip for main stem, eight 6 x ½in (15 x 1.2cm) strips for small stems
- White tissue paper: 6 cuff pieces (cuff pattern 4, p189)
- Blue tissue paper: 36 small petal pieces and 15 large petal pieces, 6 small petals per bloom and 5 large petals for 3 of the blooms to make them fuller (petal patterns 20 and 21, p183)
- Light green card stock: 2 leaves (leaf pattern 21, p172)

TECHNIQUES:

- **5:** Making centers—cuffed single pip stamen
- **4:** Petal styling—scrunching
- **8:** Attaching petals—single petals (arrange 6 small petals evenly around the cuffed center of each bloom, then evenly add 5 large petals to 3 of the blooms to make them fuller)
- **7:** Making leaves—card stock leaves
- **10:** Covering stems
- **12:** Attaching extra stems—spike (arrange the 3 smaller blooms at the top of the spike, then the larger blooms, ending with the leaves at the bottom of the sequence)
- **13:** Styling leaves and stems

Gladiolus

YOU WILL NEED:

- Four gray single pip stamens on 4½in (11cm), 22-gauge (0.65mm) wire stems
- Two 4½in (11cm), 22-gauge (0.65mm) wire stems for buds
- One 18in (46cm), 18-gauge (1mm) wire for main stem
- Light green tissue paper: one 20 x ½in (50 x 1.2cm) strip for main stem, six 6 x ½in (15 x 1.2cm) strips for small stems
- Light yellow tissue paper dipped in bleach: 6 small petal pieces, 3 petals each for 2 buds, and 24 large petal pieces, 6 petals each for 4 blooms (petal patterns 20 and 21, p183)
- Light green card stock: 2 leaves (leaf pattern 14, p170)

TECHNIQUES:

- **2:** Paper bleaching—dipped
- **5:** Making centers—single pip stamen
- **4:** Petal styling—scrunching
- **8:** Attaching petals—single petals (arrange three large petals evenly around each stamen center, then arrange three large petals evenly around the first layer of petals for each bloom)
- **4:** Petal styling—rolled curling for outer petals (use your fingers to curl the outer three petals on each bloom)
- **6:** Making berries and buds—petaled buds (use three small petals for each bud)
- **7:** Making leaves—card stock leaves
- **10:** Covering stems
- **11:** Attaching leaves—card stock leaves
- **12:** Attaching extra stems—spike (arrange the two petaled buds at the top of the spike, then add the four blooms along the stem)
- **13:** Styling leaves and stems

Canna

YOU WILL NEED:

- Three burgundy single pip stamens on three 4½in (11cm), 20-gauge (0.8mm) wire stems
- Two 6in (15cm), 20-gauge (0.8mm) wires for leaf stems
- One 18in (46cm), 18-gauge (1mm) wire for main stem
- Burgundy tissue paper: one 20 x ½in (50 x 1.2cm) strip for main stem, five 6 x ½in (15 x 1.2cm) strips for small stems, and 5 petal pieces (petal pattern 20, p183)
- Orange tissue paper dipped in water: 15 small and large petal pieces, 5 petal pieces of each size per small bloom (petal patterns 20 and 21, p183)
- Burgundy card stock: 2 leaves (leaf pattern 16, p171)

TECHNIQUES:

- **1:** Paper dyeing—using water (for orange petals)
- **5:** Making centers—single pip stamen
- **4:** Petal styling—scrunching
- **8:** Attaching petals—single petals (arrange five small petals evenly around the stamen center, then arrange 5 large petals evenly around the small petals for each bloom)
- **4:** Petal styling—rolled curling (use your fingers to curl the large petals on each bloom)
- **7:** Making leaves—card stock leaves
- **10:** Covering stems
- **11:** Attaching leaves—tissue paper leaves (for attaching the burgundy petals along the main stem)
- **12:** Attaching extra stems—spike (arrange the burgundy tissue paper leaves and blooms at the top of the main stem, adding the card stock leaves at the bottom)
- **13:** Styling leaves and stems

Hyacinth

YOU WILL NEED:

- Eight 4½in (11cm), 22-gauge (0.65mm) wire stems
- One 9in (23cm), 18-gauge (1mm) wire for main stem
- Light green tissue paper: one 12 x ½in (30 x 1.2cm) strip for main stem
- Purple tissue paper: eight 6 x ½in (15 x 1.2cm) strips for small stems, 8 small petal pieces, 1 petal piece per small bloom (petal pattern 11, p180)
- Purple crepe paper: 4 large petal pieces to fill space along the main stem (petal pattern 12, p180)
- Light green card stock: 2 leaves (leaf pattern 51, p178)

TECHNIQUES:

- **4:** Petal styling—scrunching
- **8:** Attaching petals—continuous petals (attach the small petals at the end of the small wire stems or cover the tip of the wire with matching tissue paper and allow a small portion of the wire to show like a stamen. Cut the large petal sections in half and arrange the petals along the main stem using the same technique)
- **4:** Petal styling—scissor curling for all small and large petals
- **7:** Making leaves—card stock leaves
- **10:** Covering stems
- **11:** Attaching leaves—card stock leaves
- **12:** Attaching extra stems—spike (Attach a small bloom to the top of the main stem, then add a section of large petals below the bloom to fill in space and create a fuller shape, then add the next bloom, and another section of large petals; repeat with the remaining pieces)
- **13:** Styling leaves and stems

Flower Chain

PROJECT

TECHNIQUES:

• pages 162–163

Floral Crown

PROJECT

TECHNIQUES:

• pages 164–165

Scarlet Sage

YOU WILL NEED:

- Eight 4½in (11cm), 22-gauge (0.65mm) wire stems
- Three 4½in (11cm), 22-gauge (0.65mm) wires for leaf stems
- One 9in (23cm), 18-gauge (1mm) wire for main stem
- Green tissue paper: one 12 x ½in (30 x 1.2cm) strip for main stem, eleven 6 x ½in (15 x 1.2cm) strips for small stems
- Red tissue paper: 8 small petal pieces, 1 petal piece per small bloom (petal pattern 11, p180)
- Red crepe paper: 2 large petal pieces to fill space at top of main stem (petal pattern 12, p180)
- Green card stock: 3 leaves (leaf pattern 13, p170)

TECHNIQUES:

- **4:** Petal styling—scrunching
- **8:** Attaching petals—continuous petals (attach the small petals at the end of the small wire stems or cover the tip of the wire with matching tissue paper and allow a small portion of the wire to show like a stamen. Cut the large petal sections in half and arrange the petals along the main stem using the same technique)
- **4:** Petal styling—scissor curling for all small and large petals
- **7:** Making leaves—card stock leaves
- **10:** Covering stems
- **12:** Attaching extra stems—spike (attach a small bloom to the top of the main stem and add a section of large petals below the bloom to fill in space and create a fuller shape, then add the next bloom and another section of large petals, continuing with the next two blooms and large petal pieces; place the last three blooms spaced further down the main stem)
- **13:** Styling leaves and stems

Bells of Ireland

YOU WILL NEED:

- Seven light yellow single pip stamens on seven 4½in (11cm), 22-gauge (0.65mm) wire stems
- Two 4½in (11cm), 22-gauge (0.65mm) wires for leaf stems
- One 18in (46cm), 18-gauge (1mm) wire for main stem
- Light green tissue paper: one 12 x ½in (30 x 1.2cm) strip for main stem, nine 6 x ½in (15 x 1.2cm) strips for small stems
- Light green tissue paper: 7 petal pieces (petal pattern 24, p184)
- Green card stock: 2 leaves (leaf pattern 20, p172)

TECHNIQUES:

- **5:** Making centers—single pip stamen
- **8:** Attaching petals—bell petals
- **7:** Making leaves—card stock leaves
- **10:** Covering stems
- **12:** Attaching extra stems—spike (attach one bloom to the top of the main stem and arrange the rest of the blooms in pairs along the length of the main stem with the leaves at the bottom)
- **13:** Styling leaves and stems

Daffodil

YOU WILL NEED:

- One pale yellow triple pip stamen on a 9in (23cm), 18-gauge (1mm) wire stem
- Light green tissue paper: one 12 x ½in (30 x 1.2cm) strip for main stem
- Yellow tissue paper or crepe paper: 1 petal piece for center (petal pattern 26, p184)
- Light yellow tissue paper dipped in bleach: 12 petal pieces, 2 pieces per petal (petal pattern 25, p184)
- Light green card stock: 2 leaves (leaf pattern 51, p178)

TECHNIQUES:

- **2:** Paper bleaching—dipped (for the outer petals)
- **5:** Making centers—multiple pip stamen
- **8:** Attaching petals—bell petals (for the center petal piece)
- **4:** Petal styling—pleating (for the outer double petals)
- **8:** Attaching petals—double petals (arrange the first three double petals evenly around the bell petal center, then fill in the spaces with the last three double petals)
- **7:** Making leaves—card stock leaves
- **10:** Covering stems
- **11:** Attaching leaves—card stock leaves
- **12:** Attaching extra stems—single bloom
- **13:** Styling leaves and stems

Fritillaria

YOU WILL NEED:

- Three burgundy single pip stamens on three 4½in (11cm), 22-gauge (0.65mm) wire stems
- One 15in (38cm), 18-gauge (1mm) wire for main stem
- Green tissue paper: one 20 x ½in (50 x 1.2cm) strip for main stem, three 6 x ½in (15 x 1.2cm) strips for small stems
- Burgundy tissue paper dipped in bleach: 3 petal pieces (petal pattern 27, p184)
- Green card stock: 2 leaves (leaf pattern 51, p178)

TECHNIQUES:

- **2:** Paper bleaching—dipped
- **5:** Making centers—single pip stamen
- **8:** Attaching petals—bell petals
- **4:** Petal styling—rolled curling for petal tips
- **7:** Making leaves—card stock leaves
- **10:** Covering stems
- **11:** Attaching leaves—card stock leaves
- **12:** Attaching extra stems—spike
- **13:** Styling leaves and stems

Lily of the Valley

YOU WILL NEED:

- Ten light yellow single pip stamens on ten 4½in (11cm), 22-gauge (0.65mm) wire stems
- Three 4½in (11cm), 22-gauge (0.65mm) wires for leaf stems
- Two 12in (30cm), 18-gauge (1mm) wires for main stems
- Light green tissue paper: two 15 x ½in (38 x 1.2cm) strips for main stem, thirteen 6 x ½in (15 x 1.2cm) strips for small stems
- White tissue paper: 10 petal pieces, 1 piece per small bloom (petal pattern 32, p185)
- Light green card stock: 3 leaves (leaf pattern 7, p169)

TECHNIQUES:

- **5:** Making centers—single pip stamen
- **8:** Attaching petals—bell petals
- **7:** Making leaves—card stock leaves
- **10:** Covering stems
- **12:** Attaching extra stems—spike
- **13:** Styling leaves and stems

Foxglove

YOU WILL NEED:

- Twelve burgundy single pip stamens on twelve 4½in (11cm), 22-gauge (0.65mm) wire stems
- Three clay buds on three 4½in (11cm), 22-gauge (0.65mm) wire stems
- Two 4½in (11cm), 22-gauge (0.65mm) wires for leaf stems
- One 18in (46cm), 18-gauge (1mm) wire for main stem
- Green tissue paper: one 20 x ½in (50 x 1.2cm) strip for main stem, seventeen 6 x ½in (15 x 1.2cm) strips for small stems
- Hot pink tissue paper dipped in bleach with burgundy paint speckling: three 2 x 2in (5 x 5cm) pieces for buds, 6 small and 6 large petal pieces (petal patterns 28 and 29, p184)
- Green card stock: 2 leaves (leaf pattern 8, p169)

TECHNIQUES:

- **2:** Paper bleaching—dipped
- **3:** Paper painting—watercolor or acrylic ink speckling
- **5:** Making centers—single pip stamen
- **8:** Attaching petals—bell petals
- **6:** Making berries and buds—oblong clay buds
- **7:** Making leaves—card stock leaves
- **10:** Covering stems
- **12:** Attaching extra stems—spike (arrange the three clay buds at the top of the spike, then the six smaller blooms, followed by the larger blooms, ending with the leaves at the bottom of the sequence)
- **13:** Styling leaves and stems

Harebell

YOU WILL NEED:

- Three yellow single pip stamens on thee 4½in (11cm), 22-gauge (0.65mm) wire stems
- Three 4½in (11cm), 22-gauge (0.65mm) wire stems for buds
- One 15in (38cm), 18-gauge (1mm) wire for main stem
- Light green tissue paper: one 20 x ½in (50 x 1.2cm) strip for main stem, six 6 x ½in (15 x 1.2cm) strips for small stems and 6 leaves (leaf patterns 29 and 30, p173)
- Light purple tissue paper: three 1 x 10in (2.5 x 25cm) strips for buds and 3 petal pieces (petal pattern 27, p184)

TECHNIQUES:

- **5:** Making centers—single pip stamen
- **8:** Attaching petals—bell petals
- **4:** Petal styling—rolled curling for petal tips
- **6:** Making berries and buds—rolled paper buds
- **7:** Making leaves—small tissue paper leaves
- **10:** Covering stems
- **11:** Attaching leaves—tissue paper leaves
- **12:** Attaching extra stems—spike (begin with attaching one bud to the top of the spike and then adding a bloom; continue alternating along the length of the main stem)
- **13:** Styling leaves and stems

Portulaca Grandiflora

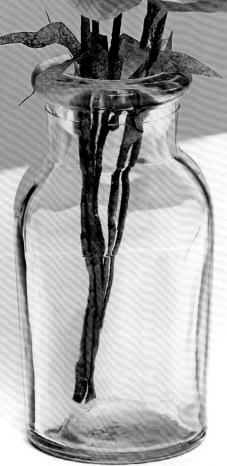

YOU WILL NEED:

- One 9in (23cm), 20-gauge (0.8mm) wire stem
- Light brown tissue paper: one 12 x ½in (30 x 1.2cm) strip for main stem
- Green tissue paper: 6 to 8 leaves (leaf patterns 29 and 30, p173)
- Golden yellow tissue paper: one 2 x 3in (5 x 7.5cm) piece for small fringed center
- Golden yellow, red, or hot pink tissue paper dipped in bleach: 2 petal pieces (petal pattern 9, p180)

TECHNIQUES:

- **2:** Paper bleaching—dipped
- **5:** Making centers—small fringe center
- **4:** Petal styling—scrunching
- **8:** Attaching petals—continuous petals (arrange the first petal piece evenly around the center, then add the second petal piece evenly behind the first)
- **7:** Making leaves—small tissue paper leaves
- **10:** Covering stems
- **11:** Attaching leaves—tissue paper leaves
- **12:** Attaching extra stems—single bloom
- **13:** Styling leaves and stems

Primrose

YOU WILL NEED:

- Three single cotton swab centers on three 9in (23cm), 20-gauge (0.8mm) wire stem
- Five 4½in (11cm), 20-gauge (0.8mm) wires for leaf stems
- Green tissue paper: three 12 x ½in (30 x 1.2cm) strip for main stems, five 6 x ½in (15 x 1.2cm) strips for leaf stems
- Light yellow tissue paper: three 2 x 2in (5 x 5cm) pieces for cotton swab centers
- White tissue paper dipped in pink dye: 6 petal pieces, 2 pieces per small bloom (petal pattern 9, p180)
- Green card stock: 5 leaves (leaf pattern 44, p176)

TECHNIQUES:

- **1:** Paper dyeing—dyeing white tissue paper
- **5:** Making centers—single cotton swab center
- **4:** Petal styling—scrunching
- **8:** Attaching petals—continuous petals (arrange the first petal piece evenly around the center, then add the second petal piece evenly behind the first)
- **7:** Making leaves—card stock leaves
- **10:** Covering stems
- **12:** Attaching extra stems—cluster (attach all 5 leaves directly below the cluster of blooms, joining each stem at the same height)
- **13:** Styling leaves and stems

Hellebore

YOU WILL NEED:

- One 9in (23cm), 20-gauge (0.8mm) wire stem
- One 4½in (11cm), 20-gauge (0.8mm) wire for leaf stem
- Green tissue paper: one 12 x ½in (30 x 1.2cm) strip for main stem, one 6 x ½in (15 x 1.2cm) strip for leaf stem
- Light yellow tissue paper: one 2 x 3in (5 x 7.5cm) piece for small fringed center
- Light green tissue paper with burgundy paint speckling: 2 petal pieces (petal pattern 9, p180)
- Green card stock: 1 leaf (leaf pattern 46, p176)

TECHNIQUES:

- **5:** Making centers—small fringe center
- **3:** Paper painting—watercolor or acrylic ink speckling
- **4:** Petal styling—scrunching
- **8:** Attaching petals—continuous petals (arrange the first petal piece evenly around the center, then add the second petal piece evenly behind the first)
- **7:** Making leaves—card stock leaves
- **10:** Covering stems
- **12:** Attaching extra stems—single bloom
- **13:** Styling leaves and stems

Mallow

YOU WILL NEED:

- Three single cotton swab centers on three 4½in (11cm), 22-gauge (0.65mm) wire stems
- Three 4½in (11cm), 22-gauge (0.65mm) wire for leaf stems
- One 9in (23cm), 18-gauge (1mm) wire for main stem
- Light green tissue paper: one 12 x ½in (30 x 1.2cm) strip for main stem, six 6 x ½in (15 x 1.2cm) strips for small stems
- White tissue paper: three 2 x 2in (5 x 5cm) pieces for cotton swab centers
- Light purple tissue paper dipped in bleach with fuchsia painted stripes: 3 petal pieces, one piece per small bloom (petal pattern 9, p180)
- Light green card stock: 3 leaves (leaf pattern 19, p172)

TECHNIQUES:

- **2:** Paper bleaching—dipped
- **3:** Paper painting—acrylic craft paint stripes
- **5:** Making centers—single cotton swab center
- **4:** Petal styling—scrunching
- **8:** Attaching petals—continuous petals
- **7:** Making leaves—card stock leaves
- **10:** Covering stems
- **12:** Attaching extra stems—spike
- **13:** Styling leaves and stems

Wood Poppy

YOU WILL NEED:

- One cotton swab center on a 9in (23cm), 20-gauge (0.8mm) wire stem
- Two 4½in (11cm), 20-gauge (0.8mm) wires for leaf stems
- Light green tissue paper: one 12 x ½in (30 x 1.2cm) strip for main stem, two 6 x ½in (15 x 1.2cm) strips for leaf stems
- Light yellow tissue paper: one 2 x 2in (5 x 5cm) piece for cotton swab center
- Golden yellow tissue paper: one 2 x 3in (5 x 7.5cm) piece for small fringed center
- Yellow tissue paper dipped in water: 2 petal pieces (petal pattern 9, p180)
- Light green card stock: 2 leaves (leaf pattern 24, p173)

TECHNIQUES:

- **1:** Paper dyeing—using water
- **5:** Making centers—single cotton swab center
- **5:** Making centers—small fringe center
- **4:** Petal styling—scrunching
- **8:** Attaching petals—continuous petals (arrange the first petal piece evenly around the center, then add the second petal piece evenly behind the first)
- **7:** Making leaves—card stock leaves
- **10:** Covering stems
- **12:** Attaching extra stems—single bloom
- **13:** Styling leaves and stems

Petunia

YOU WILL NEED:

- One single cotton swab center on one 9in (23cm), 20-gauge (0.8mm) wire stem
- Green tissue paper: one 12 x ½in (30 x 1.2cm) strip for stem and 4 leaf pieces (leaf patterns 38 and 39, p175)
- Light yellow tissue paper: one 2 x 2in (5 x 5cm) piece for cotton swab center
- Red tissue paper with bleached stripes: 2 petal pieces (petal pattern 13, p181)

TECHNIQUES:

- **2:** Paper bleaching—stripes
- **5:** Making centers—single cotton swab center
- **4:** Petal styling—scrunching
- **8:** Attaching petals—continuous petals (arrange the first petal piece halfway around the center, then fill in other side with the next petal piece)
- **7:** Making leaves—small tissue paper leaves
- **10:** Covering stems
- **11:** Attaching leaves—tissue paper leaves
- **12:** Attaching extra stems—single bloom
- **13:** Styling leaves and stems

Hibiscus

YOU WILL NEED:

- One 9in (23cm), 18-gauge (1mm) wire stem
- One 4½in (11cm), 20-gauge (0.8mm) wire for leaf stem
- Green tissue paper: one 10 x ½in (25 x 1.2cm) strip for stem, one 6 x ½in (15 x 1.2cm) strip for leaf stem
- Red tissue paper: one 6 x ½in (15 x 1.2cm) strip for stamen section of the wire stem
- Light yellow tissue paper: one 2 x 5in (5 x 12cm) piece for small bottlebrush center
- Red or hot pink tissue paper dipped in bleach: 10 petal pieces (petal pattern 15, p181)
- Green card stock: 1 leaf (leaf pattern 34, p175)

TECHNIQUES:

- **2:** Paper bleaching—dipped
- **5:** Making centers—bottlebrush center (cover the wire stem with red tissue paper strip first, then add the yellow piece just below the top, allowing the red tip of the wire to show)
- **4:** Petal styling—scrunching
- **8:** Attaching petals—double petals (be sure to attach each double petal working in a clockwise sequence around the bloom)
- **7:** Making leaves—card stock leaves
- **10:** Covering stems
- **12:** Attaching extra stems—single bloom
- **13:** Styling leaves and stems

Hollyhock

YOU WILL NEED:

- Three single cotton swab centers on three 4½in (11cm), 22-gauge (0.65mm) wire stems
- Three clay buds on three 4½in (11cm), 22-gauge (0.65mm) wire stems
- Two 4½in (11cm), 22-gauge (0.65mm) wires for petaled buds
- Six 4½in (11cm), 22-gauge (0.65mm) wires for leaf stems
- Two 18in (46cm), 18-gauge (1mm) wire stems taped together for extra stable main stem
- Light green tissue paper: one 20 x ½in (50 x 1.2cm) strip for main stem, fourteen 6 x ½in (15 x 1.2cm) strips for smaller stems, and three 2 x 2in (5 x 5cm) pieces for clay buds
- Light yellow tissue paper: three 2 x 2in (5 x 5cm) pieces for cotton swab centers
- Golden yellow tissue paper: 3 cuff pieces for cotton swab centers (cuff pattern 5, p189)
- Light pink tissue paper with pink painted stripes: 16 small petals, 2 petaled buds with 3 petals each, 2 open blooms with 5 petals each, and 5 large petals for the largest open bloom (petal patterns 14 and 15, p181)
- Light green card stock: 6 leaves (leaf pattern 19, p172)

TECHNIQUES:

- **3:** Paper painting—acrylic craft paint stripes
- **5:** Making centers—cuffed single cotton swab center
- **4:** Petal styling—scrunching
- **8:** Attaching petals—single petals (arrange 5 single petals evenly around each of the 3 cotton swab centers to create 2 smaller blooms and 1 larger bloom)
- **6:** Making berries and buds—oblong clay buds
- **6:** Making berries and buds—petaled buds
- **7:** Making leaves—card stock leaves
- **10:** Covering stems
- **12:** Attaching extra stems—spike (arrange the three clay buds at the top of the spike, then the two petaled buds, then the two smaller blooms, followed by the large bloom; pair two leaves with each bloom and attach the leaves behind the blooms, one on each side)
- **13:** Styling leaves and stems

Trumpet Flower

YOU WILL NEED:

- Three single cotton swab centers on three 4½in (11cm), 22-gauge (0.65mm) wire stems
- Three 4½in (11cm), 22-gauge (0.65mm) wires for leaf stems
- One 9in (23cm), 18-gauge (1mm) wire for main stem
- Light green tissue paper: one 12 x ½in (30 x 1.2cm) strip for main stem and six 6 x ½in (15 x 1.2cm) strips for smaller stems
- Golden yellow tissue paper: three 2 x 2in (5 x 5cm) pieces for cotton swab centers
- Coral tissue paper dipped in water: 3 petal pieces, 1 piece per bloom (petal pattern 13, p181)
- Light green card stock: 3 leaves (leaf pattern 13, p170)

TECHNIQUES:

- **1:** Paper dyeing—using water
- **5:** Making centers—single cotton swab center
- **4:** Petal styling—scrunching
- **8:** Attaching petals—continuous petals
- **4:** Petal styling—rolled curling using fingers to shape petal edges
- **7:** Making leaves—card stock leaves
- **10:** Covering stems
- **12:** Attaching extra stems—cluster
- **13:** Styling leaves and stems

Morning Glory

YOU WILL NEED:

- Three single cotton swab centers on three 4½in (11cm), 22-gauge (0.65mm) wire stems

- Two 4½in (11cm), 22-gauge (0.65mm) wires for petaled buds

- Five 4½in (11cm), 22-gauge (0.65mm) wires for leaf stems

- Five 9in (23cm), 22-gauge (0.65mm) wire stems for tendrils

- Two 18in (46cm), 18-gauge (1mm) wires taped together for main stem

- Green tissue paper: one 20 x ½in (50 x 1.2cm) strip for main stem, ten 6 x ½in (15 x 1.2cm) strips for smaller stems, and five 12 x ½in (30 x 1.2cm) strips for tendril stems

- Golden yellow tissue paper: three 2 x 2in (5 x 5cm) pieces for cotton swab centers

- Blue tissue paper with bleached stripes: 4 petal pieces, 3 open blooms with 1 petal piece each, and 2 petaled buds made from 1 petal piece cut in half (petal pattern 13, p181)

- Green card stock: 5 leaves, 2 small, 2 medium, and 1 large (leaf patterns 10, 11, and 12, p170)

TECHNIQUES:

- **2:** Paper bleaching—stripes
- **5:** Making centers—single cotton swab center
- **4:** Petal styling—scrunching
- **8:** Attaching petals—continuous petals
- **6:** Making berries and buds—petaled buds
- **7:** Making leaves—card stock leaves
- **10:** Covering stems
- **11:** Attaching leaves—card stock leaves
- **12:** Attaching extra stems: tendrils and spike (attach the blooms and buds in random order along the length of the main stem, alternating with leaves and tendrils added at the same joint with the main stem)
- **13:** Styling leaves and stems

Olive Branch

YOU WILL NEED:

- Fifteen 3in (7.5cm), 32-gauge (0.2mm) wires for leaf stems
- One 18in (46cm), 20-gauge (0.8mm) wire for main stem
- Sage green tissue paper: one 20 x ½in (50 x 1.2cm) strip for main stem, fifteen 5 x ½in (12 x 1.2cm) strips for leaf stems
- Sage green and light sage green card stock: 7 small leaves and 8 large leaves (leaf patterns 4 and 5, p168)

TECHNIQUES:

- **7:** Making leaves—card stock leaves
- **10:** Covering stems
- **12:** Attaching extra stems—spike (attach 1–2 small leaves to the top of the wire stem, then disperse the rest of the leaves at random, pairing a few leaves at a single joint along the main stem)
- **13:** Styling leaves and stems

Honey Locust Stem

YOU WILL NEED:

- Thirteen 3in (7.5cm), 32-gauge (0.2mm) wires for leaf stems
- One 18in (46cm), 20-gauge (0.8mm) wire for main stem
- Golden yellow tissue paper: one 20 x ½in (50 x 1.2cm) strip for main stem, thirteen 5 x ½in (12 x 1.2cm) strips for leaf stems
- Golden yellow card stock: 7 small leaves and 6 large leaves (leaf patterns 4 and 5, p168)

TECHNIQUES:

- **7:** Making leaves—card stock leaves
- **10:** Covering stems
- **12:** Attaching extra stems—spike (attach 1 small leaf to the top of the wire stem, then 2 pairs of small leaves, then add the 3 pairs of large leaves, followed by the last pair of small leaves)
- **13:** Styling leaves and stems

Eucalyptus

YOU WILL NEED:

- One 15in (38cm), 20-gauge (0.8mm) wire stem
- Sage green tissue paper: one 20 x ½in (50 x 1.2cm) strip for stem
- Sage green card stock: 9 small leaves and 4 to 6 large leaves (leaf patterns 49 and 50, p178)

TECHNIQUES:

- **7:** Making leaves—card stock leaves
- **10:** Covering stems
- **11:** Attaching leaves—tissue paper leaves (use the tissue paper leaves method for these small card stock leaves; glue the small stem to the wire stem and cover with tissue paper strip for added security)
- **12:** Attaching extra stems—spike (attach one small leaf to the top of the wire stem and arrange the rest of the leaves in pairs along the length, being sure to join the leaf pairs at alternating directions)
- **13:** Styling leaves and stems

Mistletoe

YOU WILL NEED:

- Seven 9in (23cm), 20-gauge (0.8mm) wire stems
- Fourteen white clay berries
- Green tissue paper: seven 12 x ½in (30 x 1.2cm) strips for stems
- Green card stock: 7 leaves (leaf pattern 41, p176)

TECHNIQUES:

- **6:** Making berries and buds—round clay berries (attach the berries last, glueing them at the stem joints and dispersing them at random)
- **3:** Paper painting—alcohol-based marker (add small black dot on mistletoe berries)
- **7:** Making leaves—card stock leaves
- **10:** Covering stems
- **12:** Attaching extra stems—spike (create all joints approximately 1in (2.5cm) apart, begin by creating three "Y" stems, then attach these three stems together to form a branch, and add the last single stem at the bottom of the branch arrangement)
- **13:** Styling leaves and stems

Pussy Willow

YOU WILL NEED:

- One 18in (46cm) foraged tree branch
- Six white clay buds

TECHNIQUES:

- **6:** Making berries and buds—oblong clay buds
- **12**: Attaching extra stems—branch

Calla Lily

YOU WILL NEED:

- Three clay oblong centers on 9in (23cm), 20-gauge (0.8mm) wire stems
- Three 4½in (11cm), 20-gauge (0.8mm) wire for leaf stems
- Green tissue paper: three 12 x ½in (30 x 1.2cm) strips for main stems, three 6 x ½in (15 x 1.2cm) strips for leaf stems
- Light yellow tissue paper: three 2 x 2in (5 x 5cm) pieces for clay centers
- White tissue paper: 3 double petals made from 2 petals attached together (petal pattern 1, p178)
- Green card stock: 3 leaves (leaf pattern 7, p169)

TECHNIQUES:

- **5:** Making centers—oblong clay center
- **7:** Making leaves—large tissue paper leaves (use to create the petal)
- **8:** Attaching petals—bell petals (when creating the bell shape, curl the rounded lobes of the petal piece around the wire, with the tip of the petal piece at the top edge)
- **4:** Petal styling—scissor curling for the point of the petal
- **7:** Making leaves—card stock leaves
- **10:** Covering stems
- **12:** Attaching extra stems—single bloom
- **13:** Styling leaves and stems

Prayer Plant

YOU WILL NEED:

- One 15in (38cm), 18-gauge (1mm) wire stem
- Green tissue paper: one 20 x ½in (50 x 1.2cm) strip for stem
- Olive green card stock: 1 leaf (leaf pattern 1, p168)

TECHNIQUES:

- **3:** Paper painting—painting card stock leaves and colored pencil
- **7:** Making leaves—card stock leaves
- **10:** Covering stems
- **13:** Styling leaves and stems

Making
the
Flowers

Materials & Tools

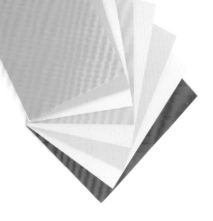

The materials and tools listed here can be bought at craft stores or online. Making paper flowers is not a craft that should break the bank—I use household items when I can, and ask friends and family to keep tissue paper from gifts for me. Some of these materials and tools are required to complete the projects while others are not essential but are wonderful additions to your crafting tool kit.

ESSENTIAL MATERIALS

Tissue paper
Most of the flowers are made with regular gift-wrapping tissue paper, which creates lifelike petals. I like to paint, dye, bleach, or dip the paper in water to create unique blooms.

Card stock
Card stock is used for most leaves and comes in many colors with smooth or textured surfaces.

Glue
Most of the projects in this book can be completed using simple white tacky craft glue.

Modeling clay
This is used for centers, berries, buds, and seedpods. A lightweight clay adds volume to the flower but not much weight. Try Crayola Model Magic, which requires no baking.

Cotton balls and swabs
Cotton balls can be used for buds, berries, seedpods, and centers. Swabs can be cut in half and covered with tissue paper to create centers for some flowers.

Pips
Pips are used to create delicate stamens and come in a range of shapes, colors, and sizes.

Floral wire
This is used for flower stems. I prefer floral wire wrapped in thread, which comes in 18in (46cm) lengths; I cut the wire in half to create two 9in (23cm) flower stems. My most-used wire is 20-gauge (0.8mm); I use 22-gauge (0.65mm) wire for smaller stems, and 18-gauge (1mm) wire for larger flowers or long stems. For wired petals I use 32-gauge (0.2mm) white floral wire.

OPTIONAL MATERIALS

Crepe paper
This adds textural interest or can be used instead of tissue paper.

Floral tape
I usually cover stems with strips of tissue paper, but floral tape is a good alternative and is easy to use.

Sealer glue finish
A glossy sealer glue finish can be used to stick two layers of tissue paper together or to create a glossy finish on card stock leaves. My preferred brand is Mod Podge.

Paint or ink
Acrylic craft paint can be used to decorate tissue paper or card stock. Add water acrylic craft paint to control the opacity. Watercolor paint and acrylic ink create softer, coloring than acrylic craft paint.

Dye
A variety of dyes can be used: fabric dye, Easter egg dye, food coloring, diluted acrylic ink, watercolor paint, or various homemade natural dyes.

Markers
Water-based markers are used to create markings on paper and bleed when you add water. Alcohol-based markers can also be used and do not bleed when you add water.

Household bleach
Bleach diluted with water can be used for dipping tissue paper.

Florist's foam
Florist's foam comes in sheets or blocks and is used for securing flower stems in a vase or pot.

TOOLS

Hot glue gun
Using a hot glue gun is the easiest way to attach card stock leaves to the main stem and is useful if you incorporate non-paper materials, such as fabric, wool, and yarn, in your projects.

Wire cutters
A pair of wire cutters from a tool set will be perfectly adequate or you can use specialist floral wire cutters.

Scissors
Paper-cutting or crafting scissors are the best options. A pair of scissors with longer blades is useful for cutting smooth curves; cutting paper close to the fulcrum will give you the most control. Keep your scissors sharp to prevent tearing. Fringing scissors are a wonderful investment if you make large quantities of paper flowers.

Ruler and rotary cutter
These are not essential, but they make cutting tissue paper into strips easier and quicker since they allow you to cut up to six layers of paper at once.

Cutting mat
It's helpful to work on a flat, smooth work surface, especially when rolling modeling clay into shapes; I cover mine with butcher's paper.

Paintbrushes
A medium-sized brush with soft bristles is the most versatile, but it is good to have a variety of brushes to create different effects.

Paper-scoring tool
The back of a knife blade or a bone-folding tool can be used to create a crease for veins on a card stock leaf.

Before You Start

If you are new to paper flower crafting, I recommend reading through the techniques in this section first to get a good idea of the steps and processes for creating your own paper garden. Once you have a grasp of the techniques, you can put your own spin on the steps, substitute materials, and play with different finishing touches—this is how I create new flower specimens and varieties.

CUTTING TIPS

Most packaged tissue paper comes in sizes 20 x 20in (50 x 50cm) or 20 x 26in (50 x 66cm) which I cut into 3in (7.5cm), 4in (10cm), or 5in (12cm) strips for petals. To create small strips of tissue to cover stems, the most precise method is to layer six sheets of tissue paper on a cutting mat and cut using a rotary cutter and steel ruler. Fold one sheet of tissue paper in half four times along the same side, then make ½in (1.2cm) parallel cuts beginning at one edge of the folded sheet. This can also be done freehand with scissors if you don't have a rotary cutter.

When cutting the tissue paper into the shapes needed, I always fold multiple layers of tissue together depending on how many pieces I need per project. I keep a good grasp on the stack as I cut the shapes freehanded, which gives organic and uneven edges. You could also clip the layers together along the bottom edge with the template on top of the stack; this will let you cut a very precise shape and gives you the chance to cut quite a few pieces if you are making large quantities.

GLUEING AND TAPING TIPS

You can use floral tape or tissue paper to cover stems. I enjoy using strips of tissue paper glued to the floral wire because the colors are more vibrant than floral tape, which is usually a darker, more muted green color.

Always apply glue in a thin layer. As you work with the tissue paper, it should feel damp, but not soggy. If the tissue paper is too saturated with glue, then it will tear. When working with multiple layers of petals, I recommend allowing the glue to dry before adding the next layer of petals to prevent the bloom from becoming lopsided. If the flower gets too heavy before the glue dries completely the wet glue and gravity will cause the petals to sag, resulting in a slightly oblong-shaped blossom.

When using floral tape the trick to making it stick to itself is to stretch the tape as you go to activate the adhesive. When using floral tape, I precut several 2–3in (5–7.5cm) sections before assembling the flower.

BLEACHING, DYEING, AND PAINTING TIPS

Since this process can get messy, I work over a sheet of plastic and wear clothing I don't mind getting dirty. The key to achieving good results is to have your space set up to allow you to move quickly from bleaching, painting, and dyeing to drying.

The most efficient method of drying tissue paper that has been bleached or dyed is to hang it from a drying rack or wire hangers hung above a sheet of plastic. Laying the tissue paper directly on a flat surface covered in plastic works, too, although the paper will dry more slowly using this method. When painting tissue paper or card stock, leave the paper flat until the paint has dried, or you may end up with drip marks and smears.

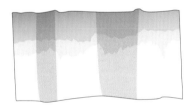

Assembling tip

Make several flowers at once. I usually work in batches of four to ten flowers at a time, which makes the process much faster. Working in an assembly-line fashion also gives the glue a chance to dry between steps while you are working.

Technique 1

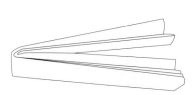

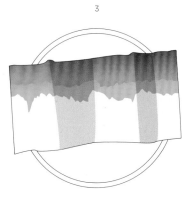

Dip-dyed tissue paper

Water-dipped tissue paper

Dyed colored tissue paper

Paper dyeing

There are various types of dye you can use for paper flowers, including Easter egg dye, food coloring, sugar-free Kool-Aid powder (or a generic equivalent), diluted acrylic ink, fabric dye, watercolor, paint, and various homemade natural dyes. Experiment with different recipes to create unique tissue paper colors. For dyeing tissue paper, follow the package instructions on the dye or just add water a little at a time until you find a color you like.

YOU WILL NEED

6 sheets tissue paper (white or colored)

Dye of your choice

Water (optional)

STEP 1 Stack six sheets of tissue paper together and fold lengthwise like an accordion, then fold the stack in half. Your bundle should easily fit into the container of dye. I like the bundle to be about 2in (5cm) wide in order to get consistent coloring.

STEP 2 Take your bundle and dip approximately 1in (2.5cm) of the cut end of the paper into the solution for five seconds. Then lift it out of the solution and let the excess liquid drip off the bundle.

STEP 3 Carefully unfold the bundle, but do not try to separate the sheets of tissue paper until the stack is dry.

STEP 4 Hang the stack of tissue paper to dry, or lay it out flat. Once the tissue paper is completely dry, carefully separate the sheets.

Tip

I find that some forms of coloring will fade over time, but I like the soft, muted colors that develop. For the most permanent color I recommend using a fabric dye.

Additional techniques

Try dyeing using water only. Although the color of your tissue paper will remain unaffected, the smooth paper will develop a lovely crinkled texture.

Dyeing white tissue paper is a great way to create bicolored flowers. Dip-dye one end of the paper for a dark-to-light ombré effect or dye each end in complementing colors for multicolored petals.

You can also dip already-colored tissue paper in a darker shade to create a deeper gradient.

Technique 2

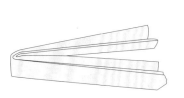

x2

x1

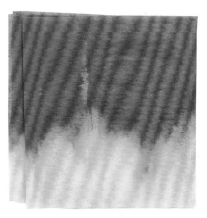

Bleach-dipped tissue paper

Bleach stripe effect

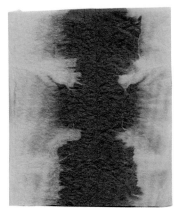

Paper bleaching

When using bleach, it is important to make sure that your space is well ventilated and the bleach is kept away from any surfaces that could be potentially damaged by spills or splatters. Dipping colored tissue paper into a bleach solution is a neat process to watch, but keep in mind that when you dip the paper it will not always change color immediately. Also, some colors will not necessarily turn white or a lighter shade of that color when bleached. Black paper can turn brown, yellow, or orange; green paper will usually turn a shade of aqua blue, while some orange and brown colors will turn pink or peach.

YOU WILL NEED

Household bleach

Water

Glass bowl

6 sheets colored tissue paper

STEP 1   To prepare the bleach solution, carefully mix one tablespoon of household bleach into two cups of cold water in a glass bowl (make sure the bowl and spoon are not used for food). Some tissue paper brands and types react to bleach differently, so you may need to adjust the bleach solution or dipping time.

STEP 2   Stack six sheets of tissue paper together and fold lengthwise like an accordion, then fold the stack in half. Your bundle should easily fit into the bowl. I like the bundle to be about 2in (5cm) wide to get consistent bleaching.

STEP 3   Take your bundle and dip approximately 1in (2.5cm) of the cut end of the paper into the solution for five seconds. Then lift it out of the solution and let the excess liquid drip off the bundle.

STEP 4   Carefully unfold the bundle, but do not try to separate the sheets of tissue paper until the stack is dry.

STEP 5   Hang the stack of tissue paper to dry, or lay it out flat. Once the tissue paper is completely dry, carefully separate the sheets.

Additional technique

To create a striped effect, repeat step 2 making sure to accordion-fold the stack of tissue paper but try not to crease the folds. Then dip one folded side of the bundle approximately 1in (2.5cm) into the solution for 5 seconds. For slightly thinner stripes, dip each folded side of your bundle ½in (1.2cm) into the solution for 5 seconds.

Tip

Dip for a few seconds longer or add a little more bleach for a more defined color gradient. Dip for less time or further dilute your bleach solution for a softer color gradient.

Technique 3

Horizontal stripes using watercolor paint

Vertical stripes using acrylic craft paint

Speckles using acrylic ink

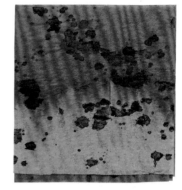

Painting petals, center color

Painting petals, full color

Painting center accents

Peony

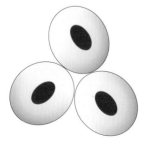

Ranunculus and borage

Poppy

Paper painting

You can use watercolors, acrylic inks, or acrylic craft paints to create beautiful painted petals and leaves. For petals, lay a single uncut sheet of tissue paper on a flat surface covered in plastic. After painting, wait for the paper to dry and then cut the sheet into strips. All of the following painting techniques can also be applied to card stock to create fun textures on leaves.

YOU WILL NEED

Selection of paints and inks

Selection of brushes

Water

Calligraphy brush

Tissue paper

Card stock

USING WATERCOLOR PAINT AND ACRYLIC INK

For soft, subtle coloring, mix watercolor paint and acrylic ink, dilute with water, and apply with a calligraphy brush.

Stripes
To create stripes, load the calligraphy brush with plenty of liquid and gently drag the brush back and forth across the paper. The more liquid that is retained in the brush the more it will bleed on the tissue paper, creating softer, irregular edges on the stripes.

Speckles
For larger, fading speckles of paint, tap the handle of the brush with your fingers approximately 10in (25cm) away from the paper.

USING ACRYLIC CRAFT PAINT

When working with acrylic craft paint on paper it is important to dilute the paint with a small amount of water to thin the consistency, otherwise the paint tends to dry with clumps.

Stripes
To get more controlled, solid stripes, use a smaller brush with plenty of paint in the brush. For a wispier texture, use a larger brush and dab some of the paint out of the brush before painting the tissue paper. I like to paint the stripes freehand, using a center fold in the paper as a guide to keep my lines fairly straight.

Speckles
To get smaller, more defined speckles use diluted acrylic paint and a larger brush; tap the brush handle with your fingers approximately 10in (25cm) away from the paper.

PAINTING PETALS

The amount of color that will show on face of the finished petal determines how much of the paper to paint.

Center color
For a streak of color in the center of a petal, apply a wide stroke or triangle of paint, beginning from the middle of the petal down to the base.

Full color
For a large swath of color paint a wide stripe down the middle of the petal.

PAINTING CENTER ACCENTS

Painting accents on flower centers adds realistic detail and gives a special touch to each handmade bloom. Cover the center with tissue paper before painting on the details.

Peony
Use red acrylic craft paint and add a small dash of paint to the tip of each cotton swab of the peony center.

Ranunculus and borage
Add a dot of dark green acrylic craft paint to the middle of the ranunculus center, or use a hole punch to create a small circle of dark green paper and glue to the center.

Poppy
Use a small paintbrush and yellow acrylic craft paint on the center of a poppy. Paint an "X" across the top of the poppy center, then add another "X" to create an asterisk on the center of the poppy.

Technique 3

Geranium and begonia leaves

Pink cordyline leaves

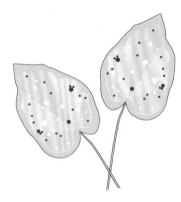

Croton leaves

Caladium leaves

Prayer plant leaves

Dusty miller leaves

PAINTING CARD STOCK LEAVES

When painting on green card stock, I prefer diluted acrylic paint to achieve the bright colors.

Geranium and begonia leaves

For geranium and begonia leaves, use a medium–small rounded brush and dab paint in a haphazard band following the edges of the leaf as a guide.

Pink cordyline leaves

For pink cordyline leaves, use the stripe method and a small rounded brush. Create "V" shapes, working from the center of the leaf toward the edges first with fuchsia, then with dark green. For a natural effect, work loosely and allow the brush to come off the paper at random spaces.

Croton leaves

For croton leaves, dab random splotches of orange and golden yellow on the paper with a small rounded brush. Then paint two columns of random dark green shapes angled toward the tip of the leaf, leaving a gap between the columns up the center of the leaf. Add a few extra splotches of dark green around the edges of the leaf.

Caladium leaves

For caladium leaves, use a medium–small rounded brush and spread paint from the center toward the edges of the leaf, leaving a gap of green showing around the edges. Then splatter with dark green and light green paint.

Prayer plant leaves

For prayer plant leaves, use a small rounded brush to paint a dark green oval in the center of the leaf. As the brush dries out, blend the edges of the oval toward the outside edges of the leaf. Use light green paint to create a thin line for the spine shape of the center of the leaf. Paint small leaf shapes on both sides of the spine, slightly offset, using the oval as a guide to start small and make the leaf shapes large in the middle and get smaller again toward the tip of the leaf. Use hot pink or fuchsia colored pencil for more control and contrast against the green colors. With the colored pencil draw a line over the light green for the vein, and add small dashes in every other light green shape. Add curved lines from the vein toward the edges, using the gap between the light green marks as a guide.

Dusty miller leaves

For dusty miller leaves, use pale sage green paint over light gray paper. Using a medium size brush, dab some of the paint out of the brush, then haphazardly create random marks all over the paper. Less paint in the brush will create a more wispy texture.

Additional techniques

Here are a few more techniques I like to use for creating special petals and leaves. These methods aren't quite as messy as paint, dye, and bleach and are great ways to add color and interest.

• Draw with colored pencil on card stock to create precise details on leaves. Colored pencils can also be used on tissue paper, but take care not to rip the paper with the pencil.

• To create vivid splotches of color, use water-soluble markers to draw designs on any type of paper, then mist the paper with water from a spray bottle. Make sure that your work surface is covered in plastic as the marker ink will run.

• Alcohol-based markers are great for creating distinct marks on any type of paper and the markings will not bleed if you use another method of coloring.

Tip

If you're using glossy card stock, apply a thin layer of paint over the entire top surface of the card stock leaf and allow to dry before scoring or assembly.

Technique 4

Scrunching

1

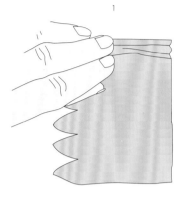

2

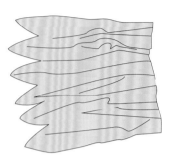

Pleating

1

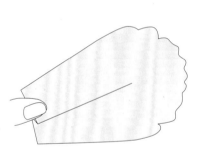

2

Pinching

1

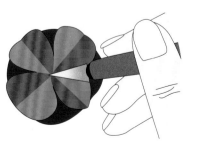

2

Petal styling

Once your tissue paper has been dyed, bleached, or painted you can get started with styling your petals. I use six simple methods for styling petals: scrunching, pleating, twisting, scissor curling, rolled curling, and cupping.

YOU WILL NEED

Tissue paper petals

Scissors

Straw or pen

SCRUNCHING

This technique can be used on any petal type to give the petals a wrinkled texture. I usually at least slightly scrunch the bottom of all the petal pieces before I begin assembling a flower because the slight wrinkles help shape the petals around the wire and also give the petals a more lifelike appearance.

STEP 1 Lay out the paper on a smooth surface. Start gently pushing the edges of the petal together, allowing the paper to bunch up under your fingers.

STEP 2 Work your way down from the top of the paper to the bottom to create an uneven, wrinkled texture.

PLEATING

Pleating is used to give petals or tissue paper leaves a cupped shape and added strength.

STEP 1 Lay out the paper on a smooth surface. In the center of the petal, gently fold the bottom of the petal over itself.

STEP 2 Crease along the fold to create a triangular-shaped dart with the top of the dart not quite reaching the top of the petal, and the base of the dart measuring approximately ¼–¾in (0.6–2cm) across.

PINCHING

This technique is used to attach petals or leaves to the wire stem after feeding the stem through a hole cut into the middle of the petal or leaf.

STEP 1 For tissue paper petals, add a small dot of glue in the center to stick multiple petal pieces together, then use a utility knife to cut a small hole in the center.

STEP 2 Feed the wire stem through the hole and add a small dot of glue at the base of the stamen, then pinch the petals around the stamen to get a ruffled effect. This technique can also be used to affix card stock leaves or petals, but I suggest using a small dot of hot glue to hold the heavier paper on the wire stem.

Tip

When pleating, a wider dart will create a more pronounced cupping of the petal. Use a dart ¾in (2cm) across the base for large petals such as peony petals. A narrower dart is helpful for strengthening thin petal and leaf shapes, such as clematis petals.

Technique 4

Scissor curling

1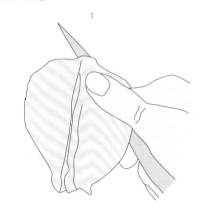

2

Rolled curling

1

2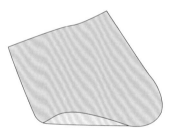

Cupping

1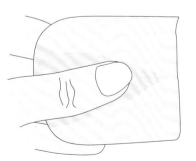

2

SCISSOR CURLING

Scissor curling petals is the same technique used for curling ribbon when wrapping gifts.

STEP 1 Place the side of the scissor's blade behind the petal and hold in place with your thumb.

STEP 2 Gently press the tissue paper with your thumb while pulling toward the edge. Apply more pressure to create a tighter curl and less pressure to create a looser curl. Experiment with curling petals forward and backward to change the look of the bloom.

ROLLED CURLING

This method can be done with a straw, a pen, or even with your own fingers.

STEP 1 Place the straw or pen at the top edge of the petal.

STEP 2 Wrap the paper around the straw or pen, taking care not to crease the petal at the edge.

CUPPING

Cupping is traditionally used with crepe paper, but I've adapted this method slightly for tissue paper petals.

STEP 1 Hold the top of the petal between the thumb and fingers of your non-dominant hand.

STEP 2 Pinch the bottom of the paper with your other hand to curve the petal around the thumb of your non-dominant hand.

Tip

Curling the petals can be done before and after assembling a flower, however, curling the petals after attaching them requires a little extra finesse to avoid tearing or creasing the tissue paper.

Technique 5

Pip stamen centers

Pip stamen centers, additional technique

1

2

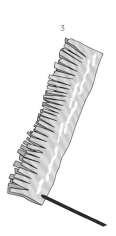

Fringe center

1

2

3

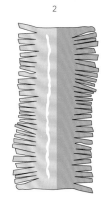

4

5

Making centers

You can create realistic-looking flower centers using pip stamens, but you can also make your own centers in a range of shapes, sizes, and colors using a variety of materials including cotton swabs, tissue and crepe paper, modeling clay, and cotton balls.

YOU WILL NEED

Tissue paper

Glue

Ready-made pip stamens

Wire stems

Cotton swabs

Scissors

Fringing scissors (optional)

Modeling clay

Cotton balls

PIP STAMEN CENTERS

Ready-made pip stamens are available online and from craft stores. Some stamens come with pips at both ends, I fold these in half and cut them to give two separate pip stamens. Pips can be attached to the flower stem with a long section of the filament showing, or cropped so that only the bulbous end of the pip is visible.

STEP 1   Using tissue paper that matches the stamen color, cut a ½ x 2in (1.2 x 5cm) strip and run two thin lines

of glue down the edges of the paper. Overlap the bottom ¼in (0.6cm) of the pip stamen with the end of a wire stem and place them together on one end of the tissue paper.

STEP 2   Working on a diagonal, fold the corner of the strip over the stamen and wire stem, sandwiching the stems between a layer of the tissue paper. Hold tightly as you twist the stems in one hand and guide the tissue paper around the wire with the other hand. Be sure to cover the joint completely to hide the tip of the wire and secure the stamen firmly.

Additional technique

To create a center with multiple pip stamens, begin with a single pip following the instructions above and repeat the process until you have as many stamens as you want. Most of the flowers with multiple pips that I create have groupings of three or six.

FRINGE CENTER

You can also create flower centers out of tissue or crepe paper. When cutting fringe for centers and stamens you can use fringing scissors or cut the fringe freehand. I've found that six to eight layers is the maximum you can cut before the paper tears instead of having a precision-cut edge.

STEP 1   Cut a rectangle of tissue paper and fold in half lengthwise, lining up the paper on the longer edge. Cut fringe approximately halfway to the fold on the non-folded edges of the long side of the tissue paper.

STEP 2   Unfold the rectangle and apply a thin line of glue following one

side of the fold, then refold the rectangle, securing the two layers of fringe together.

STEP 3   Gently bunch the strip of fringe along the fold and apply glue to the uncut half of the rectangle. Place the floral wire about ½in (0.6cm) from one end of the fringe strip.

STEP 4   Sandwich the end of the floral wire in paper, then bunch the fringe strip around the wire, while slowly spinning the wire stem.

STEP 5   Once all the paper is wrapped around the wire, fluff the fringe to give the center a more natural look.

> # Tip
>
> *For a small fringe center, cut a 2 x 3in (5 x 7.5cm) strip of tissue or crepe paper; for a medium center cut a 3 x 5in strip (7.5 x 12cm); and for a large center cut a 3 x 10in (7.5 x 25cm) strip.*

> # Tip
>
> *Fringe centers can also be combined with clay, cotton swab, or cotton ball centers for more complex centers. Create the clay, cotton swab, or cotton ball center on a wire stem first and then glue the fringe piece around the center's base, arranging the strip of fringe evenly around the center.*

Technique 5

Bottlebrush center

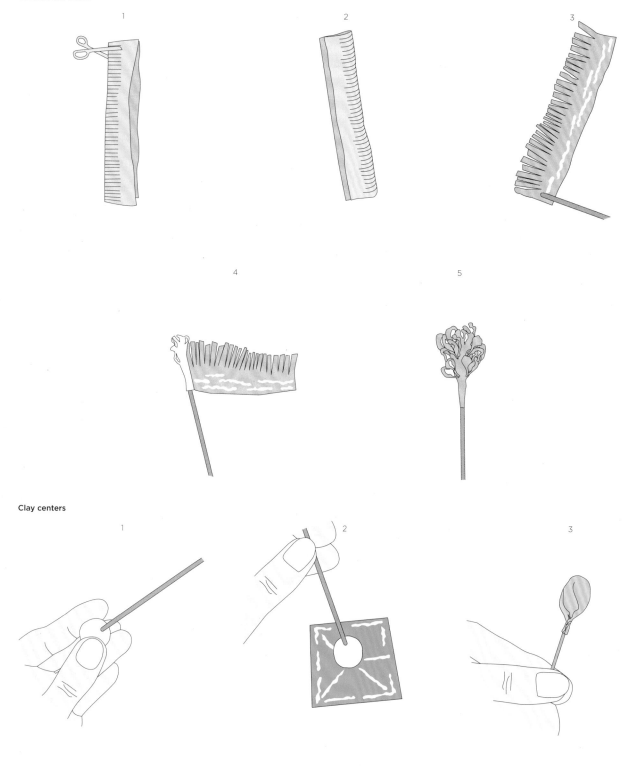

Clay centers

BOTTLEBRUSH CENTER

This method is similar to the previous technique, however, rather than cutting fringe on the unfolded edges of the rectangle, the fringe is cut on the folded edge to create a strip of loops.

STEP 1 Cut a 2 x 5in (5 x 12cm) piece of tissue paper and fold it in half lengthwise, lining up the paper on the longer edge. Cut fringe approximately halfway to the edges on the fold of the long side of the tissue paper using fringing shears, or cut the fringe freehand -using regular scissors.

STEP 2 Unfold the rectangle and apply a thin line of glue along the long side approximately ⅛in (0.4cm) from the edge, then refold the rectangle, leaving a ⅛in (0.4cm) gap between the edges. This gap creates loops along the fold.

STEP 3 Gently bunch the strip of loops along the edge and apply glue to the uncut half of the rectangle. Place the floral wire about ½in (0.6cm) from one end of the fringe strip.

STEP 4 Sandwich the end of the floral wire in paper, then bunch the strip of loops around the wire. Work at a very slight diagonal and keep the layers of loops close together, but take care not to smash them.

STEP 5 Once all the paper is wrapped around the wire, fluff the fringe to give the center a more natural look.

CLAY CENTERS

When choosing a modeling clay for paper flowers, look for one that is very lightweight, easy to mold, and dries quickly (such as Crayola's Model Magic). I prefer to use white clay for all shapes and then cover it with colored tissue paper, but you could also use colored clay and skip the tissue paper step.

STEP 1 Roll a lump of clay between your hands or on a clean, smooth work surface; leave it round or form it into the desired shape. Push a wire stem into the clay, making sure the fit is tight by spinning the base of the clay form between your fingers. Leave the clay to dry according to the packaging instructions. If the clay is loose on the stem after drying, apply a small dot of tacky glue or hot glue to the hole around the stem and allow the glue to dry before continuing.

STEP 2 Once the clay has dried, you can cover it in colored tissue paper. Take a 2 x 2in (5 x 5cm) square of tissue paper in the desired color and apply glue around the edges and middle of the paper. Press the top of the clay shape onto the center of the square.

STEP 3 Wrap the edges of the paper around the clay shape. Attach the paper to the stem firmly by pinching with your fingers.

Technique 5

Clay centers, alternative shapes

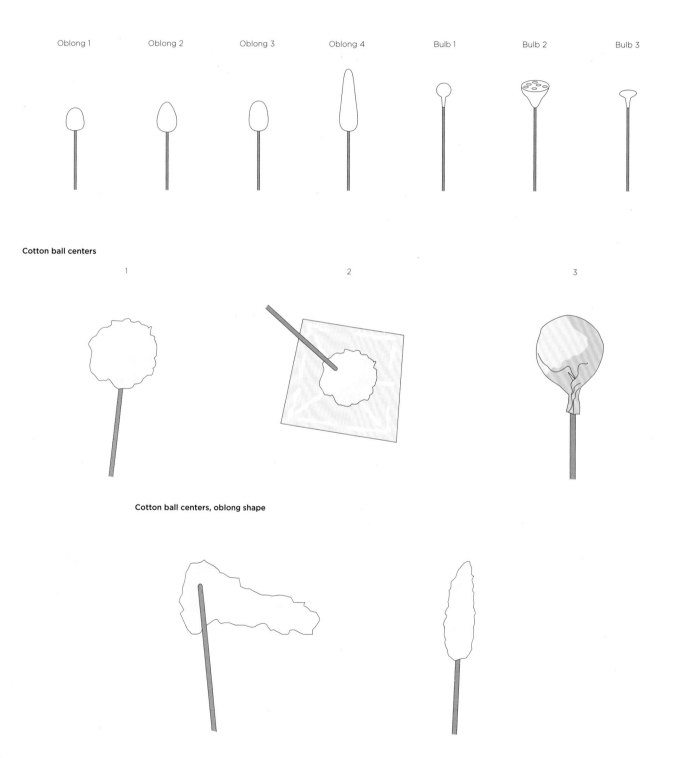

Oblong 1   Oblong 2   Oblong 3   Oblong 4   Bulb 1   Bulb 2   Bulb 3

Cotton ball centers

1   2   3

Cotton ball centers, oblong shape

Oblong centers

For an oblong center, pinch the ball of clay carefully at the top to create a plump strawberry or egg-shape. Below is a guide to different sizes of oblong centers, along with the flowers they are used for.

1. ½in (1.2cm) ball with 20-gauge (0.8mm) wire stem (ranunculus centers)

2. ¾in (2cm) ball with 20-gauge (0.8mm) wire stem (zinnia and saucer magnolia centers)

3. 1in (2.5cm) ball with 18-gauge (1mm) wire stem (black-eyed Susan and coneflower centers)

4. ¾in (2cm) ball with 20-gauge (0.8mm) wire stem (calla lily and anthurium lily centers). Form a ¾in (2cm) ball and insert the wire stem into the ball. Beginning at the tip of the wire, gently pinch and work the clay toward the bottom of the stem creating an elongated tube shape. Gently spin the clay between your fingers to smooth out any bumps and form a slight tip at the top. The clay center should measure approximately 1½in (4cm) long when finished.

Bulb centers

For a bulb center, form a ball of clay into a pear shape, then insert wire into the point of the pear and pinch to form a neck around the base of the shape. Here is a guide to different sizes of bulb centers, along with the flowers they are used for.

1. ¾in (2cm) ball with 20-gauge (0.8mm) wire stem (anemone, Iceland poppy, oriental poppy centers)

2. 1in (2.5cm) ball with 18-gauge (1mm) wire stem (waterlily pod centers). Form the bulb and flatten the top of with your fingers, then use a straw to create seed impressions across the top.

3. ½in (1.2cm) ball with 20-gauge (0.8mm) wire stem (African & shasta daisy centers). Form the bulb, then flatten it into a disc shape on the wire stem by gently pinching and molding it with your fingers.

COTTON BALL CENTERS

As a substitute for clay, cotton balls can be used for softer, more rounded centers. For large centers a full cotton ball can be used, but I prefer to unroll a ball and pull the strip of cotton into a few pieces. This allows me to create a firmer and more compact center.

STEP 1   Pull the cotton ball into several pieces, then roll them together into a ball between the palms of your hands or on a clean, smooth work surface. Take the floral wire stem and stick it into the middle of the cotton ball, twisting to allow the wire to poke through the fibers.

STEP 2   Take a 2 x 2in (5 x 5cm) square of tissue paper and apply glue around the edges and middle of the square. Press the top of the cotton shape in the center of the square.

STEP 3   Wrap the edges of the paper around the bulb and attach to the stem firmly by pinching with your fingers.

Oblong center

To create an oblong-shaped center, hold one end of a strip of cotton and wrap it tightly around the wire.

Technique 5

Cotton swab centers

1   2   3

Triple cotton swab centers

Cuffed cotton swab and pip centers

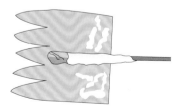

COTTON SWAB CENTERS

To create a cotton swab center, you must first determine what kind of stick the cotton swab has. Take a cotton swab and cut the stick in half. If the stick is hollow simply glue the floral wire stem directly inside the stick. The cotton swabs I use are made from rolled paper and the sticks are not hollow, which means the cotton swab must be attached to the wire with tissue paper or floral tape.

STEP 1   Before attaching a cotton swab to the wire stem, you need to cover the cotton tip with tissue paper in the desired color. To do this, apply glue to the center and around the edges of a 2 x 2in (5 x 5cm) square of tissue paper. Press the tip of the cotton swab onto the center of the square, wrap the edges down around the cotton swab, then attach to the stick firmly. If your cotton swab is hollow, you can now glue the wire stem inside the stick. If your cotton swab has a solid stick, follow steps 2 and 3.

STEP 2   Cut a ½ x 3in (0.6 x 7.5cm) strip of tissue paper (the color of this paper needs to match the tissue paper covering the cotton swab tip). Run two thin lines of glue down the edges of the paper. Overlap 1in (2.5cm) of the cotton swab stick with the end of a wire stem. Then place the floral stem and cotton swab stick together on one end of the tissue paper.

STEP 3   Working on a diagonal, fold the corner of the strip over, sandwiching the stems between a layer of the tissue paper, and hold tightly as you twist the stems in one hand and guide the tissue paper around the wire with the other hand. Be sure to cover the joint completely in order to hide the tip of the wire and to secure the cotton swab to the stem.

Additional techniques

- **Triple cotton swab centers**. Follow the instructions for a single cotton swab center but add three cotton swab halves to the wire stem one at a time to ensure that each one is attached securely. Once all three cotton swabs are attached to the wire stem, glue an additional strip of tissue paper around the bundle of cotton swab sticks and wire stem to make sure everything is secured together.

- **Cuffed centers**. Another variation is to create a cuffed center. To do this, follow the instructions for making a single cotton swab center. Cut a cuff petal piece from tissue paper, scrunch the bottom edge, and apply a thin line of glue to this edge. Arrange the cuff piece evenly around the cotton swab center, making sure to line up the top of the cuff piece with the tip of the cotton swab center. You can also wrap a cuffed piece around a pip stamen using this method.

Technique 6

Round berry 1   Round berry 2   Oblong berry 1   Oblong berry 2   Oblong berry 3

Rolled paper buds

1

2

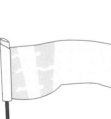

3

4

Petaled buds

1

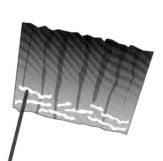

2

Making berries and buds

Berries and buds add a little extra detail and interest to your paper flower creations. You can use similar techniques and materials to make the berries and buds as you used to make the flower centers.

YOU WILL NEED

Modeling clay

Wire stems

Tissue paper

Glue

CLAY BERRIES AND BUDS

Follow the instructions for clay centers on page 135 to make berries and buds. As before, you can use white clay and cover it with colored tissue paper, or use colored clay.

Alternative shapes

• For a round berry or bud, roll a small lump of clay into a round ball between the palms of your hands or on a clean, smooth work surface. Below is a guide to different sizes of round berries and buds, along with the flowers that they are used for.

1. ½in (1.2cm) ball with 20-gauge (0.8mm) wire stem (berry stem, pokeweed and cosmos berries, daisy and dahlia buds).

2. ¼in (0.6cm) ball with no wire stem (mistletoe berries and cherry blossom buds). Press the ball gently to flatten it slightly on the back side.

• For an oblong berry or bud, pinch the ball of clay carefully at the top to create a plump strawberry or egg-shape. Below is a guide to different sizes of oblong berries and buds, along with the flowers they are used for.

1. ½in (1.2cm) ball with no wire stem (pussy willow buds). Form the clay into an egg shape, then press down gently to create a flat area on the back side of the bud to attach to the branch.

2. ¾in (2cm) ball with 20-gauge (0.8mm) wire stem (gladiolus buds).

3. 1in (2.5cm) ball with 18-gauge (1mm) wire stem (rose buds and poppy pods).

COTTON BALL BERRIES AND BUDS

As with the flower centers, cotton balls can be used for softer, more rounded berries and buds. Follow the instructions for cotton ball centers on page 137 to make the berries and buds.

ROLLED PAPER BUDS

This simple technique requires tissue paper in two colors.

STEP 1 Take a 1 x 20in (2.5 x 50cm) strip of tissue paper and apply several thin lines of glue along its length. Place the wire at one end of the paper and fold a corner of the tissue paper strip over to cover the wire end.

STEP 2 Wrap the tissue paper around the wire stem until you achieve the desired thickness and shape. The bud should measure approximately 1in (2.5cm) in length on the wire stem.

STEP 3 Use green tissue paper or floral tape to cover the stem and secure the bud. Add thin lines of glue to the paper and overlap it approximately ⅛in (0.4cm) over the bottom of the bud.

STEP 4 Shape the bud by rolling it between your fingers and then bend it slightly.

PETALED BUDS

Petaled buds have no center or stamen; instead the petals are attached directly to the end of a wire stem.

STEP 1 Apply glue to the bottom edge of a tissue paper petal and lay the wire stem close to one edge.

STEP 2 Fold the edge of the petal over to hide the wire, then roll the petal around the stem to create a tight, wrinkled tube shape.

Technique 7

Card stock leaves

1

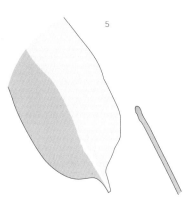

3

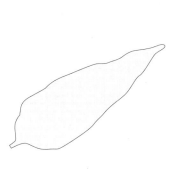

5

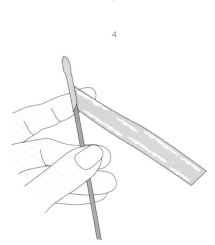

Scoring

Pronounced vein

Curling

Making leaves

Leaves are generally made from card stock, which offers a nice contrast against the tissue paper blooms and add some weight and stability to the stem. Most card stock leaves are glued onto a wire stem, which is then joined to the main flower stem. Some long, thin leaves, however, such as wheat and hyacinth are glued directly to the main stem with hot glue.

YOU WILL NEED

Card stock

Pencil

Scissors

Scoring tool

Paint

20-gauge (0.8mm) wire

Tissue paper

Glue

CARD STOCK LEAVES

STEP 1 Trace the relevant leaf template on the back of your paper with pencil. Cut out the leaf and then erase any visible pencil marks.

STEP 2 Apply paint or other decorative coloring before scoring the veins on a leaf. If the leaf will be attached directly to the main stem, then you are ready to do this, however, most card stock leaves are attached to the main stem on a wired stem.

STEP 3 To create the leaf stem, cut a 4½in (11cm) length of 20-gauge (0.8mm) wire. Cut a strip of tissue paper measuring ½ x 6in (1.2 x 15cm) and apply a thin line of glue down the length of both edges, then add a little dab of glue on both ends.

STEP 4 Firmly holding the end of the paper against an end of the wire with your thumb, fold the corner of the tissue paper over the tip of the wire and slowly twist the stem while applying pressure; guide the strip of paper with your other hand as you do this. As you work down the stem, guide the paper diagonally, making sure that the paper is wrapped tightly and overlaps. At the end of the wire, fold the tissue paper back up and over the stem, covering the end of the wire completely and twisting between your fingers firmly to attach the paper to itself.

STEP 5 Now take the card stock leaf and apply a thin line of glue on the backside following the scored vein.

STEP 6 When glueing the leaf to the wire stem make sure at least 1in (2.5cm) of the wire is glued to the leaf for added stability.

Additional techniques

Scoring a card stock leaf helps create a crease to imply veins. Take a bone-folder tool, or other paper-scoring tool, and trace vein lines on the back of the card stock leaf. Gently fold along the lines to accentuate the shape.

For a more pronounced vein than just scoring and folding the leaf provides, attach the stem on the front side of the leaf. Apply a thin line of glue on the front of the leaf following the scored line, then lay an 18in (46cm) length of tissue paper-covered wire stem on top of the glue line. Fold the leaf in half over the wire and allow to dry. After the glue dries carefully reopen the leaf to reveal the vein on the leaf. With this technique, you have the opportunity to bend the wired vein to create gentle curves in the length of the leaf to achieve a more realistic look.

Curling the edges or tips of the card stock leaves gives them extra character. To create a gentle curl use your fingers for shaping or curl leaves with the side of your scissor's blade and gently press the paper with your thumb while pulling toward the edge. For a tighter curl, roll the paper around a straw or ink pen.

TISSUE PAPER LEAVES

To create a sturdy larger leaf, stick two sheets of tissue paper together using a thin layer of glue. Once the glue has dried the leaf can be attached and styled in the same manner as card stock leaves.

For smaller leaves, cut out your leaf shape, apply a small dot of glue at the base of the leaf, then pinch the base of the leaf to attach the dot of glue to the stem.

Tip

To create veins on tissue paper leaves, simply fold the leaf down the center and crease the paper.

Technique 8

Single petals

1

2

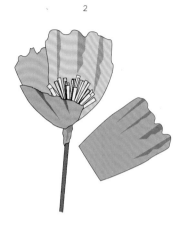

3

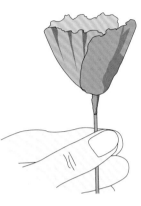

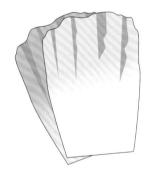

Double petals

1

2

3

Attaching petals

The petals for the flower projects in this book vary from simple single petals to more complex continuous and even wired blooms. I suggest you start by making single and double petal flowers before experimenting with the more difficult designs.

YOU WILL NEED

Ready-cut
tissue paper petals

Glue

Wire stems

SINGLE PETALS

Single petals are made from one cut petal shape.

STEP 1 Apply glue to the bottom ½in (1.2cm) of each petal. Press the glued section of the petal against the stem, directly below the center or stamen. Attach the petal to the stem as tightly as possible by pinching and twisting the base with your fingers.

STEP 2 Arrange the petals around the center or stamen evenly, slightly overlapping them as you go.

STEP 3 Once all of the petals are attached keep molding the tissue paper using a twisting motion, until the petals are secured to the stem. The base of the bloom should feel firm between your fingers.

DOUBLE PETALS

Double petals are created by stacking two cut petals of the same shape

STEP 1 Take two cut petal shapes.

STEP 2 Add a small dab of glue at the bottom edge of each petal and stick them together.

STEP 3 Add dimensionality by laying the top petal slightly askew before glueing it in place. To attach double petals to the stem, follow the instructions for attaching single petals.

Tip

When attaching single or double petals, working clockwise around the center will create a more uniform placement while placing petals randomly around the center will produce a varied, more natural look.

Technique 8

Continuous petals

1

2

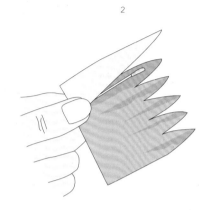

3

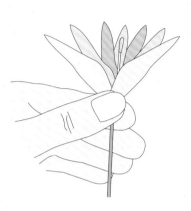

Bell petals

1

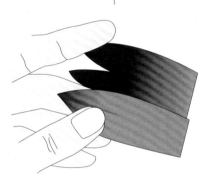

2

3

CONTINUOUS PETALS

Continuous petals are formed by a section of multiple petal shapes adjoined at the base as one piece. Continuous petals can be attached as one long length or cut into smaller sections to make attaching them easier.

STEP 1   Apply glue to the bottom ½in (1.2cm) edge of the petal section and arrange evenly around the center, or add directly to the wire stem if there is no center, while maintaining the wrinkled texture.

STEP 2   Begin attaching the petal piece at the center rather than starting at an end of the petal piece. Fold each end around the center to ensure even petal placement and to make sure the petals meet up without leaving a gap or having too much overlap.

STEP 3   At the base of the petals where the glue was applied, spin the flower firmly between your fingers to make sure all of the layers are attached securely. Use your fingers to style the individual petals to give a more natural look.

BELL PETALS

Bell petals can be a little tricky to attach, so I suggest you create a few practice pieces to help you find your favorite method for creating the right shape.

STEP 1   Begin by putting a small dot of glue on one side edge of the petal piece, then grasp the center of the petal between your thumb and index finger and curl the petal around your finger to create a tube. Secure the edges together with the dot of glue.

STEP 2   Next, slide the stem wire with or without a pip stamen center into the tube and twist the bottom ½in (1.2cm) of the petal base around the wire.

STEP 3   Put a small dab of glue on the outside of the twist and spread the glue around the twist to secure it. When sliding the bell flower off of your finger, be careful not to pull the tube of paper off the wire stem.

Tip

Instead of using your fingers to form the bell shape, you can also wrap the petal piece around the end of a marker pen. For the smallest bell flowers, such as lily of the valley, use the same process, but wrap the petal piece around a straw or ink pen cap with the stamen in the center of the straw or cap.

Technique 8

1

2

3

4

5

6

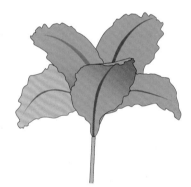

WIRED PETALS

Wired petals are great for creating definitive curves, especially in longer, thin petals when tissue paper would typically be limp. With this technique, sandwiching the wire between two cut petals hides the wire between the layers of tissue paper. Be sure to use 32-gauge (0.2mm) white floral wire or cover it with white or colored tissue paper to match the petals. Dark wire will show through the tissue paper and a heavier wire gauge will create a larger, more prominent vein down the center of the petal.

STEP 1   Apply a thin line of glue down the center of one petal piece, running from the tip to the base.

STEP 2   Lay a straight piece of floral wire on the line of glue and line up the top petal over the bottom petal, sandwiching the wire between layers. Leave a small space at the top of the petal between the edge of the petal and the tip of the wire so the wire is not exposed.

STEP 3   Allow the glued petals to dry flat before attaching them to the center. Once the petals are dry, curl the top of the wired petals back with your fingers and bend the wire at the base of the petal outward.

STEP 4   Use more tissue paper or some floral tape to cover the stem and secure the petal.

STEP 5   Once all the petals are assembled, curve them further to style the finished flower. Curl the wired petals inward toward the center to create a cupped shape.

STEP 6   Alternatively, you can curl the wired petals outward toward the base of the flower to create a more open, blooming shape.

Techniques 9 & 10

Attaching the calyx

1

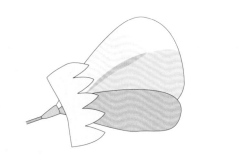

2

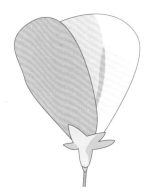

Covering stems

1

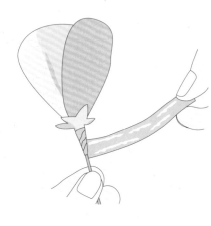

2

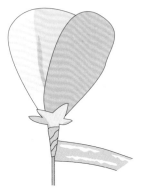

3

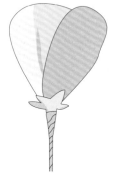

Floral tape

1

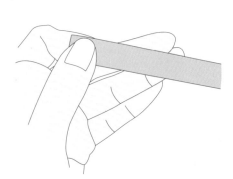

2

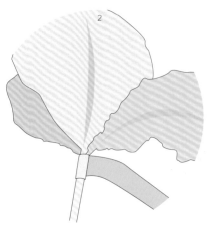

Attaching the calyx

The calyx is made of five or six sepal pieces and is positioned at the base of the flower. The technique for attaching the calyx to a paper flower is similar to that for attaching continuous petals (see page 147) because they adjoin the base as one piece.

YOU WILL NEED

Ready-cut tissue paper calyx

Glue

Paper flower

STEP 1 Apply glue to the bottom edge of the paper calyx and arrange it evenly around the base of the bloom while maintaining the wrinkled texture. Make sure that the ends of the sepal section meet to form a continuous shape.

STEP 2 At the base of the sepal section, where the glue was applied, spin firmly between your fingers to make sure that all of the layers are attached securely.

Covering stems

Whether to use tissue paper or floral tape to cover stems is purely down to personal preference. I enjoy using strips of tissue paper glued to the floral wire because the colors are typically more vibrant than floral tape, which usually has a darker, more muted green color.

YOU WILL NEED

Tissue paper

Glue

Paper flower

Floral tape

TISSUE PAPER

STEP 1 Take a ½in (1.2cm) wide strip of tissue paper and apply thin lines of glue down the length of both edges with a little dab on both ends. Beginning directly below the petals and calyx, apply the tissue paper strip to cover the stem. Firmly hold the end of the paper against the base of your bloom with your thumb and slowly twist the stem while applying pressure; guide the paper with your other hand.

STEP 2 As you work down the stem, guide the paper diagonally and make sure that the paper is wrapped tightly and overlaps.

STEP 3 At the end of the wire, fold the tissue paper back up and over the stem, covering the end of the wire completely. Twist the wire firmly between your fingers to attach the paper to itself.

FLORAL TAPE

STEP 1 The trick to making floral tape stick to itself is to stretch the tape as you go—this activates the adhesive on the tape. Firmly hold the end of the floral tape against the base of your bloom with your thumb and slowly twist the stem while applying pressure and stretching the tape with your other hand. Apply pressure to both the tape and the stem by pinching the tape against the wire between your thumb and forefinger.

STEP 2 As you work down the stem, be sure that the tape is wrapped tightly and overlaps. At the end of the wire, fold the tape back up and over the stem, covering the end of the wire completely. Twist the wire firmly between your fingers to attach the tape to itself.

Technique 11

Tissue paper leaves

1

2

Card stock leaves

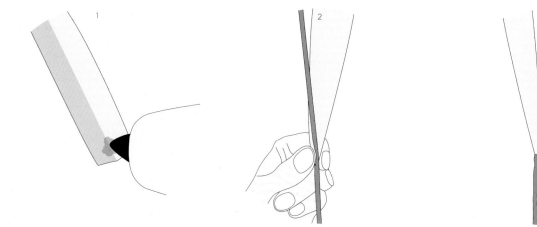

Attaching leaves

The following techniques explain how to attach both tissue paper and card stock leaves directly to a flower stem. Before glueing a leaf directly to the flower stem, pinch the base of the leaf against the stem to shape it because once the glue is dry the leaf cannot be moved at the joint. Be sure to cover the stem with tissue paper or floral tape first at the point where you want to attach the leaves.

YOU WILL NEED

Ready-cut tissue paper leaves

Glue

Paper flower

Ready-cut card stock leaves

Hot glue gun

Floral tape (optional)

TISSUE PAPER LEAVES

Take extra care when attaching tissue paper leaves; small leaves can be especially delicate.

STEP 1 Apply a small dab of glue to the base of the leaf and attach to the stem, pinching with your fingers until the glue is tacky.

STEP 2 Once attached, style the leaves with your fingers, taking care not to tear the wet tissue paper.

Tip

Try to match the leaf and stem paper colors to camouflage the join.

CARD STOCK LEAVES

When attaching card stock leaves directly to the main stem, I prefer to use my hot glue gun because it dries quickly and adds extra strength to the joint.

STEP 1 Add a small dot of hot glue at the bottom edge of the leaf.

STEP 2 Press the leaf to the stem. Be careful not to burn your fingers if any hot glue oozes out from the edge of the card stock leaf.

STEP 3 Use a small ½in (1.2cm) wide strip of tissue paper in a color that matches the rest of the stem to cover the base of the card stock leaf and any visible hot glue on the joint.

Technique 12

Attaching stems

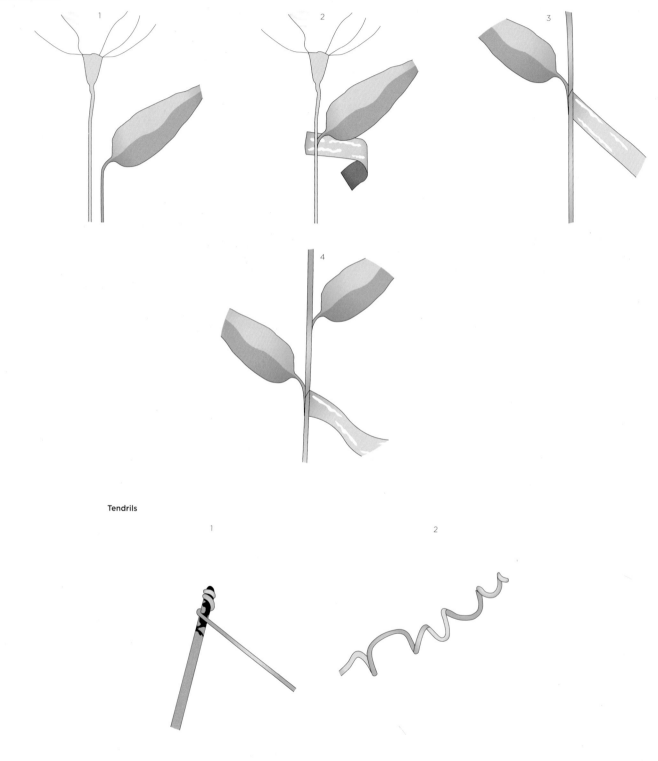

Tendrils

Attaching extra stems

Adding extra wire stems to the main stem takes some patience, but following these tips can make it much easier. First I'll cover the basic technique for adding stems before looking at how to create the various types of plant structure included in this book. Creating flowers comprised of multiple stems and smaller blooms takes time, but the results are so rewarding and truly complement large, single bloom flowers in arrangements.

YOU WILL NEED

Floral wire

Paper flowers and leaves

Tissue paper

Pencil or wooden skewer

Floral tape

Glue (if using tissue paper)

Tip

Wait until the glue on the covered stems is completely dry before styling to prevent tearing the tissue paper at the wire joints.

STEP 1   Take the additional wire with a leaf or flower at the end of it. Make a defined sharp bend in this wire facing away from the main stem; this prevents the leaf and/or flower from hindering the process.

STEP 2   Keep in mind that each stem added to the main stem should have at least 1in (2.5cm) of its own wire attached to the main stem to support its weight. To join two stems, hold both wire stems together firmly at the desired joining point with your non-dominant hand and, using the other hand, tightly wrap a 2–3in (5–7.5cm) section of ½in (1.2cm) wide glued tissue paper strip or precut floral tape to "tack" the stems together. This prevents the wires from twisting as you work, which is especially helpful when adding multiple wires to the main stem.

STEP 3   Continue wrapping the main stem with strips of tissue paper or floral tape past the point of the join to ensure that none of the bare floral wire will be visible.

STEP 4   You can also add wires to eliminate small notches in the main stem where a shorter stem does not reach the full length of the main stem. Take a straight length of wire of the same gauge as the shorter wire to extend the remaining length of the main stem. Add a small dab of glue below the shorter wire and place the new wire directly below the shorter wire as closely as possible; the glue will help hold the wires together, preventing a weakened spot. Then cover the stems with a ½in (1.2cm) wide strip of tissue paper or floral tape.

TENDRILS

As well as standard stems, you can add tendrils to your arrangements for extra decoration.

STEP 1   Take a 9in (23cm) length of 22-gauge (0.65mm) wire wrapped in tissue paper and coil it around a pencil or wooden skewer, leaving about 2in (5cm) of one end straight to attach to the main stem.

STEP 2   Remove the coiled wire and pull the ends to spread the coil apart. For a more natural appearance, play with reversing, untwisting, and bending the wire coil.

Technique 12   **Attaching extra stems**

Plant structures

Here are some ways to create plants with different types of stem, from single blooms to vines and branches.

Single bloom

This is a basic structure consisting of one flower on a main stem. I create most single bloom flowers on 9in (23cm) stems because I can get two flowers from one 18in (46cm) length of floral wire. Single blooms may have leaves attached directly to the stem or wired leaves attached to the main stem. For examples see peony (pp14–16) anemone (p34), poppy (pp35, 38, 39, 101), rose (pp44, 62, 63).

Cluster

A cluster is created by adding several stems to the top of a main stem to form a larger bloom from multiple small flowers. I use 18-gauge (1mm) wire for the primary stem to provide extra stability for the finished bloom. Begin by attaching one stem directly to the end of the primary stem, joining the pieces with ½in (1.2cm) wide strips of tissue paper; be sure to cover the stem as you work your way down. Then, working around the first bloom, add each stem one at a time to make sure the wires do not move, filling in empty spaces as you go. I hold the stem and find the placement I want, then bend the stem just above where it will join the main stem—this stops the flowers from being crushed while attaching the stems together. Once all of the stems are attached, wrap the bundle of stems a couple of extra times to make sure the cluster is secured together tightly. For examples see hydrangea (p11), rhododendron (p12), allium (p28), godetia (p40).

Spike

A spike is a tall stem with a column of multiple blooms. When working with tall stems that remain standing vertically, wrap two 18in (46cm), 18-gauge (1mm) wire stems together to provide extra stability. Begin by attaching a bud or bloom to the end of the main stem with ½in (1.2cm) wide strips of tissue paper, and add additional stems, working from top to bottom. Be sure to cover the wire stem as you work your way down. Each wire stem should be bent directly behind the bloom before joining the wire to the main stem—this makes placement easier and keeps petals from getting crushed during assembly. The main stem can be bent gently after the glue has dried. A spike can be left standing straight vertically like a hollyhock, bent in a slight, gentle curve as with freesias, or given a deeper bend to create a drooping shape, as in lilies of the valley. For examples see freesia (p72), lily of the valley (p94), foxglove (p95), hollyhock (p104).

Vine

To assemble a vine, work from the tip of the stem to the base and join the pieces with ½in (1.2cm) strips of tissue paper; be sure to cover the stem as you work your way down. Each wire stem should be bent directly behind the bloom before joining the wire to the main stem—this will help make placement easier and keeps petals from getting crushed during assembly. The main stem can be bent gently after the glue has dried. For examples see sweet pea (p24), honeysuckle (p50), sweet potato vine (p52), morning glory (p106).

Branch

I use foraged tree branches, trimmed to approximately 24in (60cm) in length and with some of the small twigs removed. Attach blooms, buds, and card stock leaves directly to the branch with a small dab of hot glue. Buds and blooms to be attached to a branch should be created without a wire stem and then trimmed at the base to provide a flat surface for the hot glue. Tissue paper leaves can be glued to the branch using tacky craft glue. For examples see dogwood branch (p43), cherry blossom branch (p46).

Single bloom   Cluster   Spike   Vine   Branch

Technique 13

Styling leaves and stems

After all the glue has dried, it's time to add the finishing touches by bending the wire stems at various angles and curves. Leaving stems straight will give your flowers an angular, rigid look. Curving the wire stems creates a more natural, relaxed style to your flowers.

YOU WILL NEED

Leaf stems

Paper flowers

Styling leaves

1

2

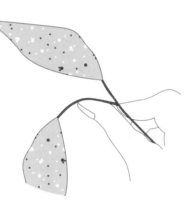

Styling stems

1

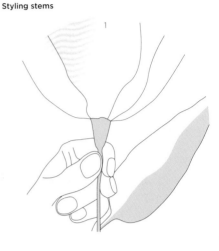

2

STEP 1   Firmly hold the wire stems directly below where the leaf stem and main stem join.

STEP 2   At the joint, bend the leaf stems out at varying angles. Then hold the leaf between your thumb and fingers and bend the wire at the point where the leaf meets the wire.

STEP 1   For single flowers, bend the stem slightly at the base of the bloom. This gives a nice view of the flower face from the top as well as the front.

STEP 2   I prefer to use my fingers to create gentle, imperfect bends and angles in the stems. However, another option is to bend the stems around bottles or jars to give the stems a more uniform curve.

Bouquet

PROJECT

Creating a bouquet can require patience as it takes time to get the flowers and stems angled exactly the way you want, but the results are definitely worthwhile. This bouquet, pictured on page 36, could serve as a beautiful and unique bridal bouquet that doubles as a keepsake or would look lovely displayed as a table-top centerpiece or decor accent. And who wouldn't love to receive a bouquet that will never wilt?

10in (26cm)

10in (26cm)

This bouquet measures approximately 10in (26cm) tall and 10in (26cm) wide

Make the following flowers and leaves:

1 Pink Hawaiian Charm Peony made from water-dipped salmon pink tissue paper with 1 large leaf and 2 small leaves on 9in (23cm), 18-gauge (1mm) wire stem

1 Iceland poppy made from bleach-dipped coral tissue paper with 2 leaves on 9in (23cm), 20-gauge (0.8mm) wire stem

1 Iceland poppy made from water-dipped pale orange tissue paper with 2 leaves on 9in (23cm), 20-gauge (0.8mm) wire stem

2 Jasmine branches made from white tissue paper (each branch has 3 blooms and 2 leaves) on 9in (23cm), 18-gauge (1mm) main stems

3 Chocolate cosmos made from water-dipped burgundy tissue paper with 1 leaf each on 3 x 15in (38cm), 20-gauge (0.8mm) wire stems

2 Fern stems made from olive green card stock on 15in (38cm), 20-gauge (0.8mm) wire stems

YOU WILL NEED

Precut 2–3in (5–7.5cm) long sections of floral tape

Wire cutters

Decorative element to cover the stems (optional)

Vase or vessel to display your bouquet (optional)

STEP 1 Begin with the largest bloom first (the peony). This provides the best visual and structural anchor for the arrangement; also, bending and arranging the smaller flower stems away from the largest bloom will help prevent it from becoming damaged or misshapen and gives the bouquet a spherical overall shape. Hold the peony in your non-dominant hand and angle the bloom slightly forward. Arrange the leaves around the face of the bloom. I usually move all of the leaves around quite a bit during the arranging process to get the best look and spacing for the bouquet. The leaves are also great for filling in any empty spots in the bouquet.

STEP 2 Add the two Iceland poppies, making a triangular shape visually. Don't be afraid to bend the stems in gentle curves pointing in various directions; not all of the flowers need to face the front and the poppies help to give the arrangement depth and color variety.

STEP 3 Attach the first piece of floral tape directly below the lowest leaf joint, pull the tape tightly as you wrap it around the three stems in your hand. You will use this piece of tape as a guide for bending and adding in the rest of the stems.

STEP 4 Next add the jasmine stems. Cluster flowers such as jasmine help to fill in negative space and create an interesting variety of textures. Secure the jasmine stems with another piece of floral tape, trying to cover the same area as the previous floral tape joint.

STEP 5 Then add the chocolate cosmos, taping the stems together in the same spot. I think of single smaller blooms as polka dots, adding several small bursts of repetitive color throughout the bouquet. I like to use this technique to infuse a darker or more vibrant contrasting hue into the color palette. Then, add in the fern stems. Group the decorative foliage stems together and bend them in varying angles to give the bouquet a more loose and natural overall feel.

STEP 6 Trim the bottom ends of the stems with wire cutters to give a more uniform base to the finished arrangement. You can also trim the stems to fit a specific vase or vessel. At this point you can either spread the stems apart below where the stems are joined with tape and leave them exposed or hold the stems all together tightly and wrap the bundled stems with floral tape down the length. Once the bouquet is formed, the floral tape joint and stems can be left bare or covered with decorative accents such as ribbon, lace, strips of fabric, twine, or leather lacing.

Tip

For the best results when creating a paper flower bouquet, I like to form the bouquet while holding the flowers in my hands, bending the stems as I go and tacking the stems together using 2–3in (5–7.5cm) sections of floral tape. The tape holds the stems together because it is slightly sticky, which makes placing stems around the bouquet easier as it gets larger.

Corsage, boutonnière & hairpin

PROJECT

Assembling a corsage is like making a miniature bouquet. I like to work with one focal flower and add several accents of single smaller blooms and a few leaves. To make a smaller version, choose one showy bloom and a single accent leaf—this gives a simple look. If you are creating a matching set or collection, use repetitive elements in each arrangement to unify the collection. When making a corsage, boutonnière, or hairpin, keep in mind that the back side of the arrangement should be flat since it will be worn against the body. Before I begin assembling the arrangement, I bend the blooms at varying angles forward. Then I like to hold the stems together in my hand, building the arrangement before I begin taping, this helps to create the tightest placement of the blooms possible and makes it easier to create a sturdy base from the stems. These beautiful corsages are pictured on page 37.

4½in (12cm)

5½in (14cm)

The corsages measure approximately 5½in (14cm) tall and 4½in (12cm) wide

For corsage A, make the following flowers and leaves:

1 Olive branch with 5 leaves made from sage and light sage card stock on 4½in (11cm), 22-gauge (0.65mm) wire stem

2 Jasmine blooms made from bleached lilac tissue paper on 4½in (11cm), 22-gauge (0.65mm) wire stems

1 Mallow bloom made from bleached lilac tissue paper with painted stripes on 4½in (11cm), 22-gauge (0.65mm) wire stem

1 Godetia bloom made from hot pink tissue paper with magenta painted stripes on 4½in (11cm), 22-gauge (0.65mm) wire stem

1 Juliet rose made from water-dipped red tissue paper with 2 leaves on 4½in (11cm), 22-gauge (0.65mm) wire stem

For corsage B, make the following flowers and leaves:

1 Olive branch with 5 leaves made from sage and light sage card stock on 4½in (11cm), 22-gauge (0.65mm) wire stem

2 Jasmine blooms made from bleached lilac tissue paper on 4½in (11cm), 22-gauge (0.65mm) wire stems

1 Mallow bloom made from bleached lilac tissue paper with painted stripes on 4½in (11cm), 22-gauge (0.65mm) wire stem

1 Godetia bloom made from water-dipped light orange tissue paper on 4½in (11cm), 22-gauge (0.65mm) wire stem

1 Juliet rose made from bleach-dipped red tissue paper with 2 leaves on 4½in (11cm), 22-gauge (0.65mm) wire stem

For corsage C, make the following flowers and leaves:

1 Olive branch with 5 leaves made from sage and light sage card stock on 4½in (11cm), 22-gauge (0.65mm) wire stem

2 Jasmine blooms made from bleached lilac tissue paper on 4½in (11cm), 22-gauge (0.65mm) wire stems

1 Mallow bloom made from bleached lilac tissue paper with painted stripes on 4½in (11cm), 22-gauge (0.65mm) wire stem

1 Godetia bloom made from bleach-dipped burgundy tissue paper on 4½in (11cm), 22-gauge (0.65mm) wire stem

1 Juliet rose made from light yellow tissue paper with red painted stripes with 2 leaves on 4½in (11cm), 22-gauge (0.65mm) wire stem

---

YOU WILL NEED

Precut 2–3in (5–7.5cm) long sections of floral tape

Wire cutters

Tip

I prefer to use floral tape to join the stems as the added wax coating on the tape makes it easier to stick a boutonnière pin or hat pin into the stem to affix the flowers to clothing.

STEP 1 Begin by holding the rose, with the stem bent forward in your non-dominant hand and arrange the leaves to your liking. You can keep adjusting the leaves as you add more stems. Next, place the godetia bloom and tape the stems together, making sure that the tape begins as close to the lowest leaf joint as possible.

STEP 2 Repeat the process, adding the mallow and jasmine blooms one at a time, filling in the negative space around the rose and godetia blooms. Finally, add the olive branch to the back of the arrangement and adjust the height to your liking before taping to the rest of the stems.

STEP 3 For a nice finishing touch, trim the bottom ends of the stems to a uniform, even length. Then cover the trimmed ends with a few more pieces of floral tape to make one clean stem.

VARIOUS FINISHES

To make a corsage, attach the arrangement to an 18in (46cm) length of 1in (2.5cm) wide ribbon with a small dab of hot glue in the center of the ribbon. Allow the hot glue to dry, then tie the ribbon around your wrist, and trim the ribbon ends to the length that you want.

To make a boutonnière, attach the arrangement to a or shirt front with a complementing boutonnière pin.

To make a hairpin, use bobby pins to secure the flower piece into the hair or insert the joined stems directly into a bun or topknot.

Flower Chain

PROJECT

This flower chain, pictured
on page 88, makes a great
decorative element for a party.
It is ideal for arranging along
a mantelpiece, or could be hung
on the wall with decorative
thumbtacks or simply placed
down the middle of a table as
a runner. The length can be
adjusted adding more flower
"links" to the chain. Several
chains can be used to create
a stunning flower curtain.

59in (150cm)

6in (15cm)

The chain measures approximately
59in (150cm) tall and 6in (15cm) wide

Make the following flowers:

3 Iceland poppies made from bleach-dipped light yellow tissue paper on 9in (23cm), 20-gauge (0.8mm) wire stems

3 Iceland poppies made from bleach-dipped light orange tissue paper on 9in (23cm), 20-gauge (0.8mm) wire stems

3 Ranunculus made from bleach-striped golden yellow tissue paper on 9in (23cm), 20-gauge (0.8mm) wire stems

3 Ranunculus made from bleach-striped hot pink tissue paper on 9in (23cm), 20-gauge (0.8mm) wire stems

5 Dinnerplate dahlias made from blush tissue paper with light pink acrylic ink stripes on 9in (23cm), 20-gauge (0.8mm) wire stems

Cut out the following leaves from various shades of green card stock, but do not attach the leaves to separate wire stems:

6 Iceland poppy leaves

6 Ranunculus leaves

5 Dinnerplate dahlia leaves

YOU WILL NEED

Craft glue

STEP 1 Before you begin assembling the flower chain, spend some time deciding on the placement you want. You can create a repetitive pattern, or random placement of blooms along the length—either way looks great! Once you've chosen the style, begin to attach the leaves, directly to the bottom end of the correlating flower stem, with a thin line of craft glue along the backside of the leaf along the scored vein. Allow the glue to dry.

STEP 2 Beginning at one end of the chain, hold the first flower in your non-dominant hand directly below the bloom. With your dominant hand bend the wire so that the wire at the bottom of the leaf meets the base of the bloom, forming a loop from the middle of the stem. Then twist the leaf stem around the base of the bloom, making sure to create at least one full twist around the base for security.

STEP 3 Next, bend the flower's stem just below the bloom to face forward, usually a 45–90° angle, but you can adjust this angle as you style the flower chain. Then shape the stem loop into a teardrop shape to allow the leaf of the next flower link to be fed through the loop.

STEP 4 When you form the next link, allow the already formed link to rest in your non-dominant hand to keep it out of the way while your dominant hand does the work of forming a loop and twisting the wire. Repeat with each bloom until the garland reaches the desired length.

STEP 5 When you hang the flower chain you may need to adjust some of the flowers due to the twisting that naturally happens when creating a chain. Simply bend the blooms and leaves at varying angles for the best placement and squeeze the loops to elongate the chain.

Floral Crown

PROJECT

This vibrant floral crown, pictured on page 89, is guaranteed to make the wearer feel extra special, great for that sweet little birthday girl you know or a most whimsical bridal accessory. Alternatively you can simply hang up the crown as a petite floral wreath. The crown is flat on one side, which will fit against the head, so it is helpful to keep in mind which side will be the top or bottom as you attach the flowers along the main stem. Be sure to attach all of the flowers to the wire stem and allow the glue to dry before bending the main stem to form the crown.

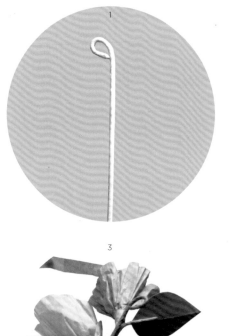

10in (26cm)

9½in (24cm)

The crown measures approximately 9½in (24cm) tall and 10in (26cm) wide

Make the following flowers and leaves on 4½in (11cm), 22-gauge (0.65mm) wire stems:

3 California poppies made from water-dipped light orange tissue paper

3 Petite camellias made from cream tissue paper

3 Zinnias made from hot pink tissue paper with magenta painted stripes

4 Morning glory blooms made from bright blue tissue paper

4 Hydrangea blooms made from light green tissue paper with burgundy speckling

8 leaves made from bright green card stock

4 leaves made from dark green card stock

(leaf pattern 37, p175, used for this project but any smaller leaves would work)

YOU WILL NEED

Precut 3in x ½in (7.5 x 1.2cm) strips of light green tissue paper

One 48in (122cm) length of ribbon for tie closure

One 18in (46cm), 18-gauge (1mm) wire stem covered in light green tissue paper

Glue

Wire cutters

STEP 1   Begin by creating a small loop at each end of the 18in (46cm) main stem wire by wrapping the end of the wire around a pencil. Make sure each loop points in the same direction.

STEP 2   Bend the wire stems of the leaves and blooms at varying angles forward or to one side—30–45° angles work well for combining these petite elements along the main stem. The angles can be adjusted later for the best fit before sticking the stems together on the main stem, then adjusted again once the flower crown is formed to be worn. Pair the leaves with some of the blooms at random or in a pattern if you prefer, and attach the stems together using 3in x ½in (7.5 x 1.2cm) strips of light green tissue paper with glue before attaching them to the main stem.

STEP 3   Starting at one end of the 18in (46cm) main stem wire, just below the loop, and working your way to the other end, space the flower and leaf stems approximately 1in (2.5cm) apart along the length of the main stem wire. Point each bloom and leaf at varying angles to nestle the flowers together as you add the stems one by one. Use the 3in x ½in (7.5 x 1.2cm) strips of tissue paper with glue to join the flower stems to the main stem. All of this could be created with floral tape, but I chose tissue paper to keep the stems as thin as possible and to prevent the crown from becoming too heavy. When you get to the end, you will need to trim some of the wire stems to just shorter than the loop at the end of the wire, then cover the wire ends with a strip of tissue paper to finish.

STEP 4   After the glue has dried completely, hold the main stem with each hand near the loops at the ends and bend the stem with flowers attached around the wearer's head or a large bowl to get a more circular shape. Thread the length of ribbon through each loop and tie a bow as a closure at the back of the head.

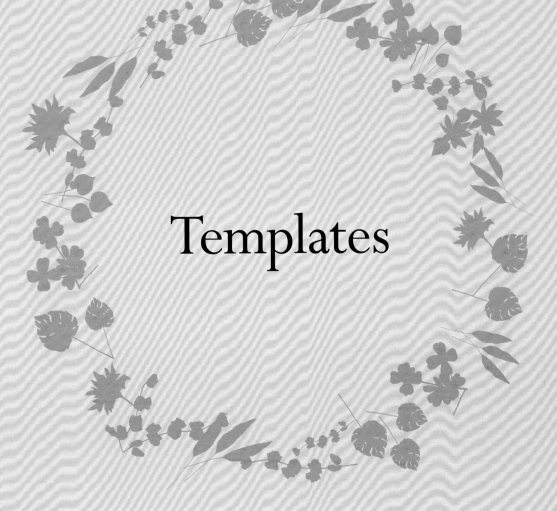

Templates

Templates

All templates are shown actual size

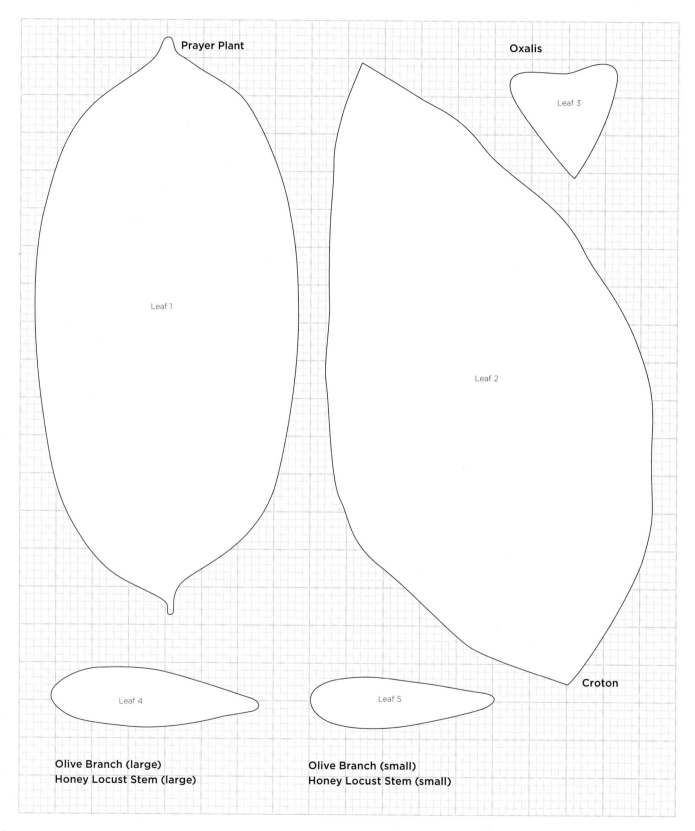

Prayer Plant

Leaf 1

Oxalis

Leaf 3

Leaf 2

Croton

Leaf 4

Leaf 5

Olive Branch (large)
Honey Locust Stem (large)

Olive Branch (small)
Honey Locust Stem (small)

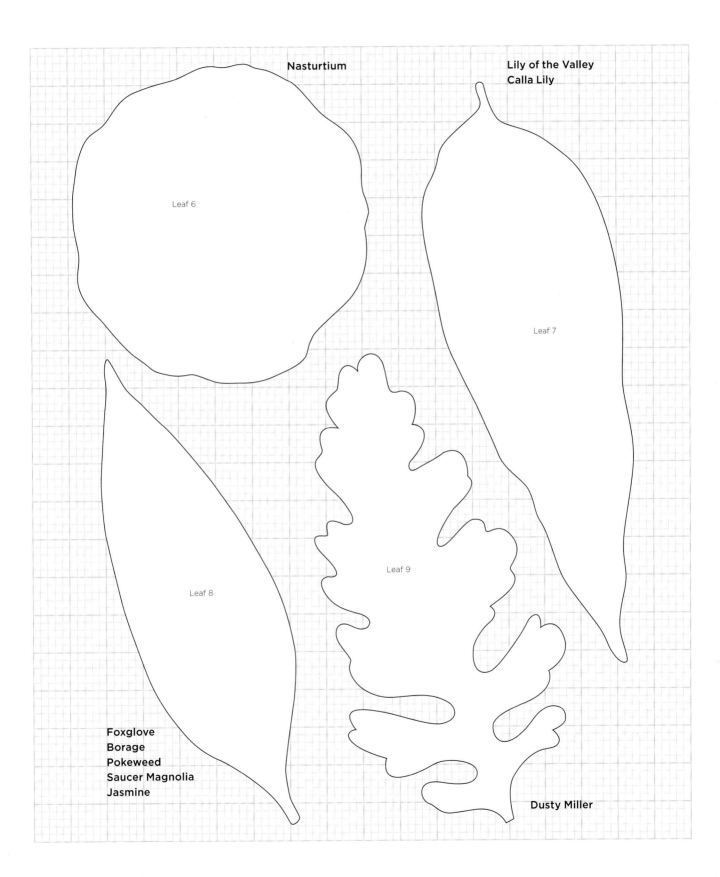

Nasturtium

Lily of the Valley
Calla Lily

Leaf 6

Leaf 7

Leaf 8

Leaf 9

Foxglove
Borage
Pokeweed
Saucer Magnolia
Jasmine

Dusty Miller

Templates

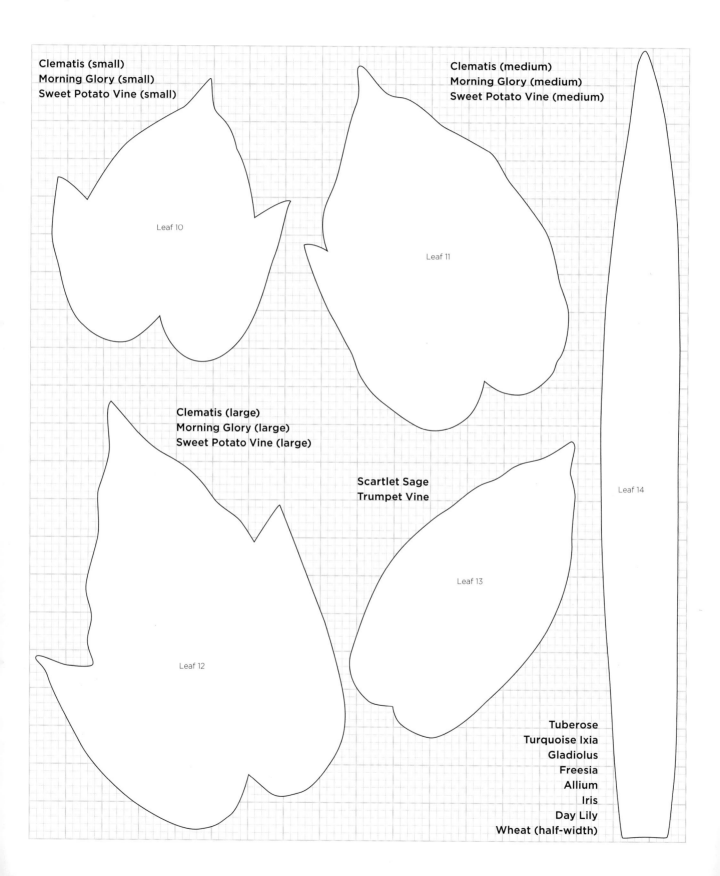

Clematis (small)
Morning Glory (small)
Sweet Potato Vine (small)

Leaf 10

Clematis (medium)
Morning Glory (medium)
Sweet Potato Vine (medium)

Leaf 11

Clematis (large)
Morning Glory (large)
Sweet Potato Vine (large)

Scartlet Sage
Trumpet Vine

Leaf 14

Leaf 13

Leaf 12

Tuberose
Turquoise Ixia
Gladiolus
Freesia
Allium
Iris
Day Lily
Wheat (half-width)

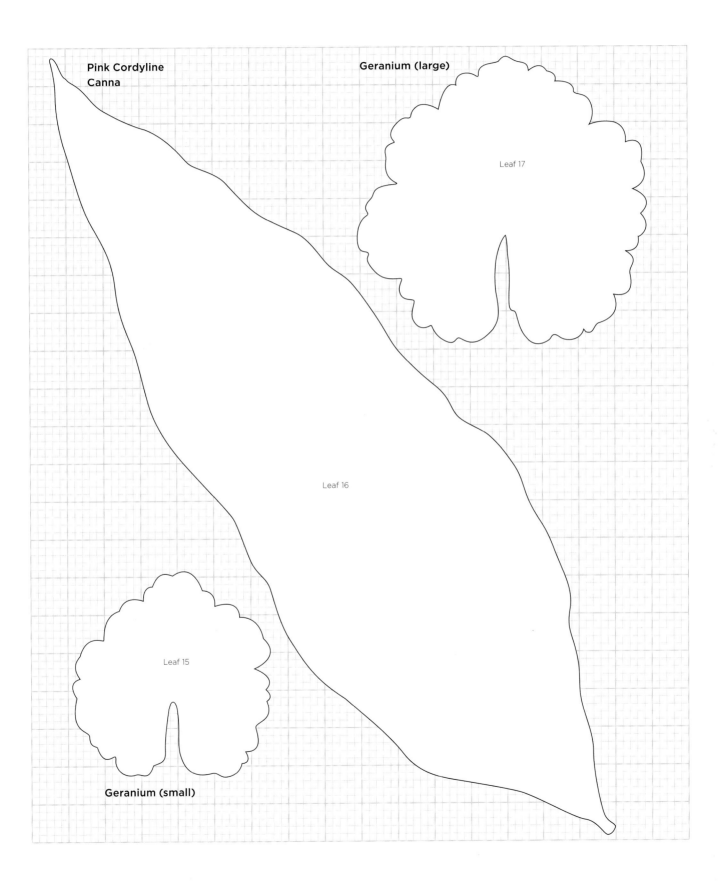

Pink Cordyline
Canna

Geranium (large)

Leaf 17

Leaf 16

Leaf 15

Geranium (small)

Templates

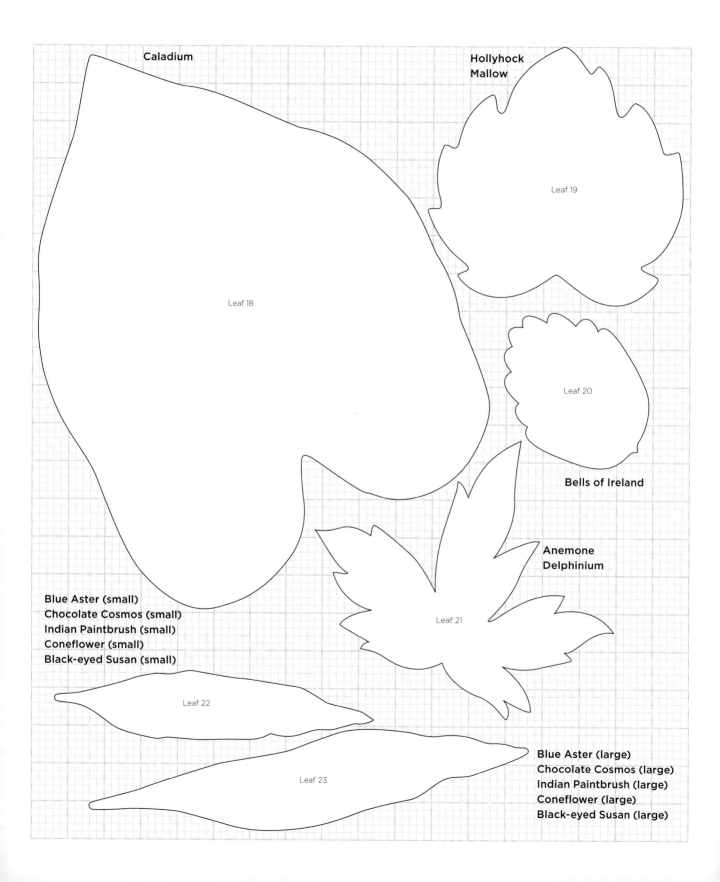

Caladium

Hollyhock Mallow

Leaf 19

Leaf 18

Leaf 20

Bells of Ireland

Anemone Delphinium

Leaf 21

Blue Aster (small)
Chocolate Cosmos (small)
Indian Paintbrush (small)
Coneflower (small)
Black-eyed Susan (small)

Leaf 22

Leaf 23

Blue Aster (large)
Chocolate Cosmos (large)
Indian Paintbrush (large)
Coneflower (large)
Black-eyed Susan (large)

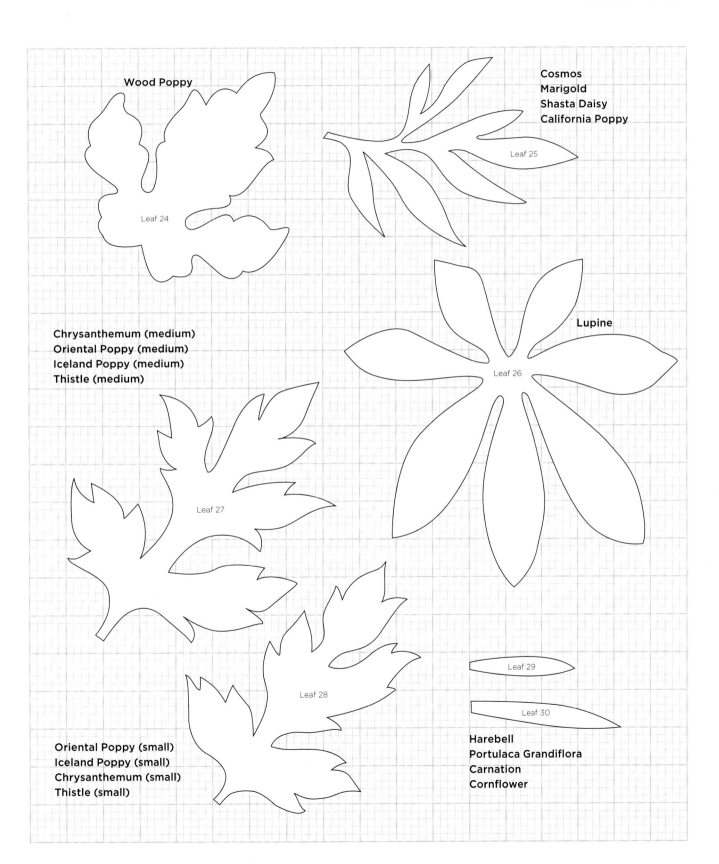

Wood Poppy

Leaf 24

Cosmos
Marigold
Shasta Daisy
California Poppy

Leaf 25

Lupine

Leaf 26

Chrysanthemum (medium)
Oriental Poppy (medium)
Iceland Poppy (medium)
Thistle (medium)

Leaf 27

Leaf 28

Leaf 29

Leaf 30

Oriental Poppy (small)
Iceland Poppy (small)
Chrysanthemum (small)
Thistle (small)

Harebell
Portulaca Grandiflora
Carnation
Cornflower

Templates

Philodendron

Leaf 31

Leaf 32

Ranuculus (small)

Leaf 33

Ranuculus (large)

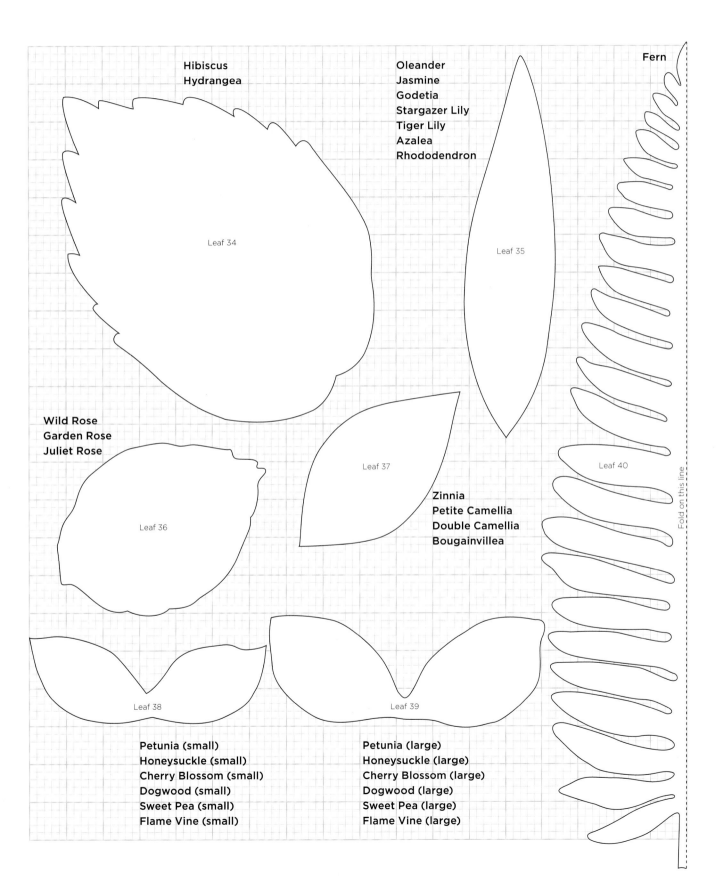

Hibiscus
Hydrangea

Oleander
Jasmine
Godetia
Stargazer Lily
Tiger Lily
Azalea
Rhododendron

Fern

Leaf 34

Leaf 35

Wild Rose
Garden Rose
Juliet Rose

Leaf 37

Leaf 40

Zinnia
Petite Camellia
Double Camellia
Bougainvillea

Leaf 36

Fold on this line

Leaf 38

Leaf 39

Petunia (small)
Honeysuckle (small)
Cherry Blossom (small)
Dogwood (small)
Sweet Pea (small)
Flame Vine (small)

Petunia (large)
Honeysuckle (large)
Cherry Blossom (large)
Dogwood (large)
Sweet Pea (large)
Flame Vine (large)

Templates

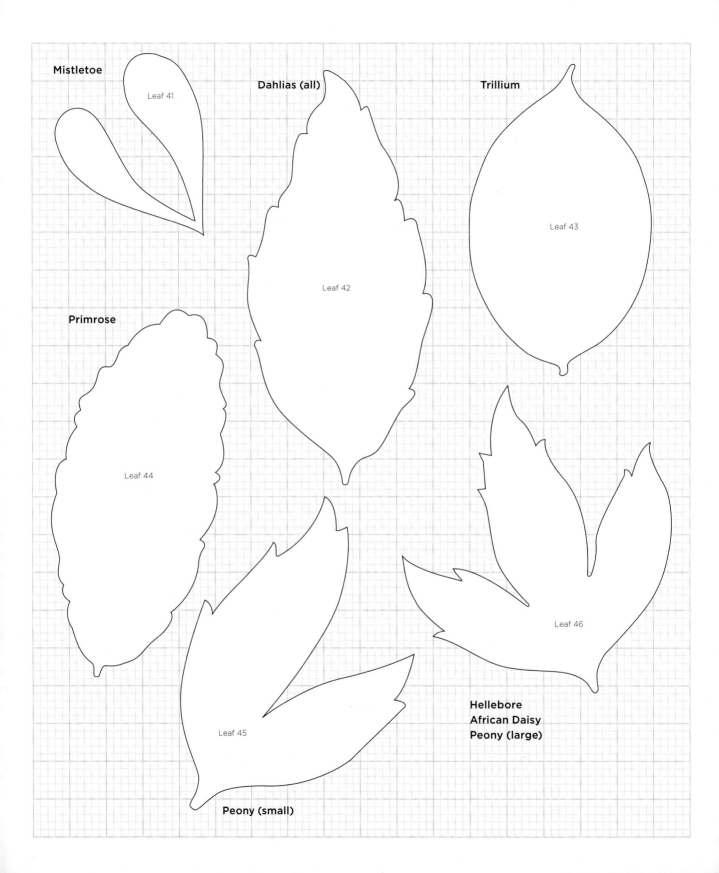

Mistletoe

Leaf 41

Dahlias (all)

Leaf 42

Trillium

Leaf 43

Primrose

Leaf 44

Leaf 46

Leaf 45

Hellebore
African Daisy
Peony (large)

Peony (small)

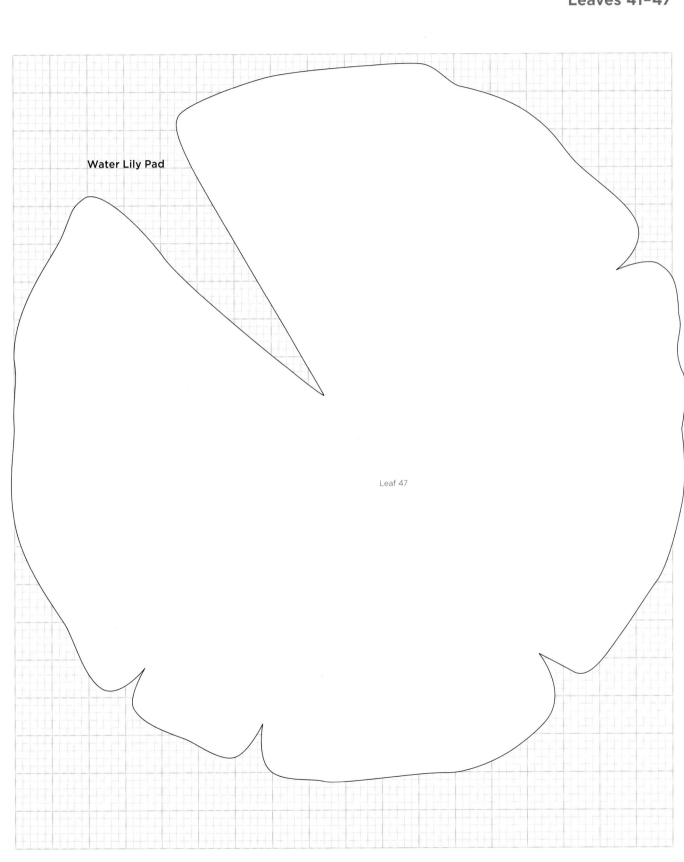

Water Lily Pad

Leaf 47

Templates

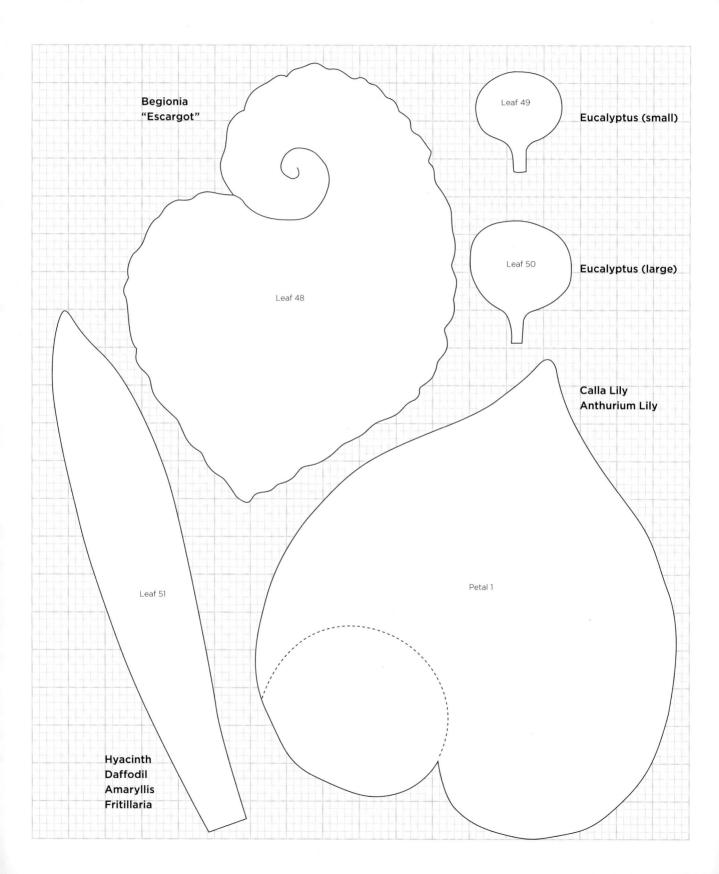

Begionia "Escargot"

Leaf 48

Leaf 49

Eucalyptus (small)

Leaf 50

Eucalyptus (large)

Calla Lily
Anthurium Lily

Petal 1

Leaf 51

Hyacinth
Daffodil
Amaryllis
Fritillaria

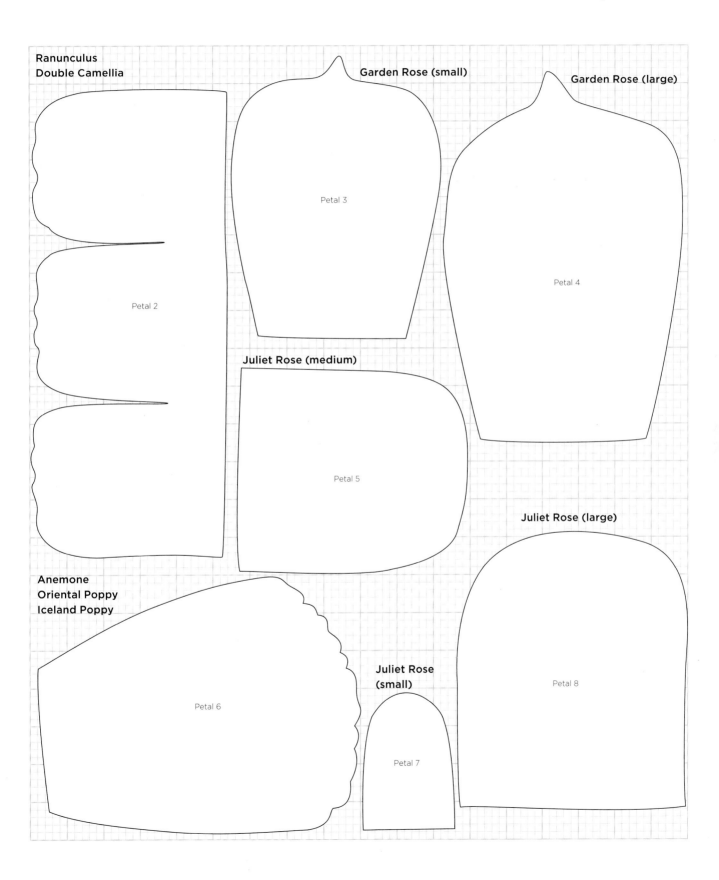

Ranunculus
Double Camellia

Garden Rose (small)

Garden Rose (large)

Petal 3

Petal 4

Petal 2

Juliet Rose (medium)

Petal 5

Juliet Rose (large)

Anemone
Oriental Poppy
Iceland Poppy

Petal 8

Petal 6

Juliet Rose
(small)

Petal 7

Templates

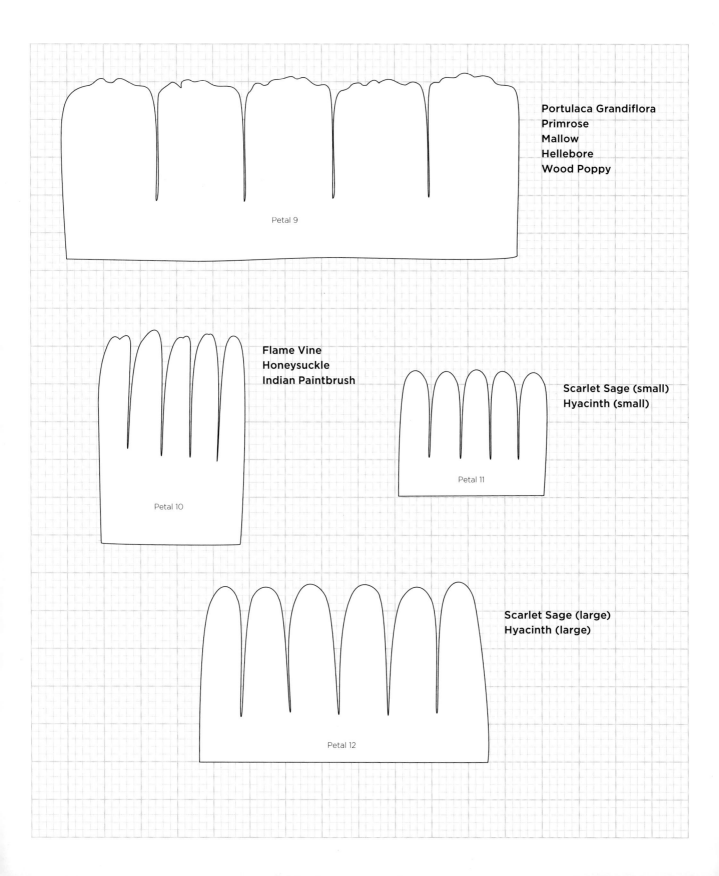

Portulaca Grandiflora
Primrose
Mallow
Hellebore
Wood Poppy

Petal 9

Flame Vine
Honeysuckle
Indian Paintbrush

Petal 10

Scarlet Sage (small)
Hyacinth (small)

Petal 11

Scarlet Sage (large)
Hyacinth (large)

Petal 12

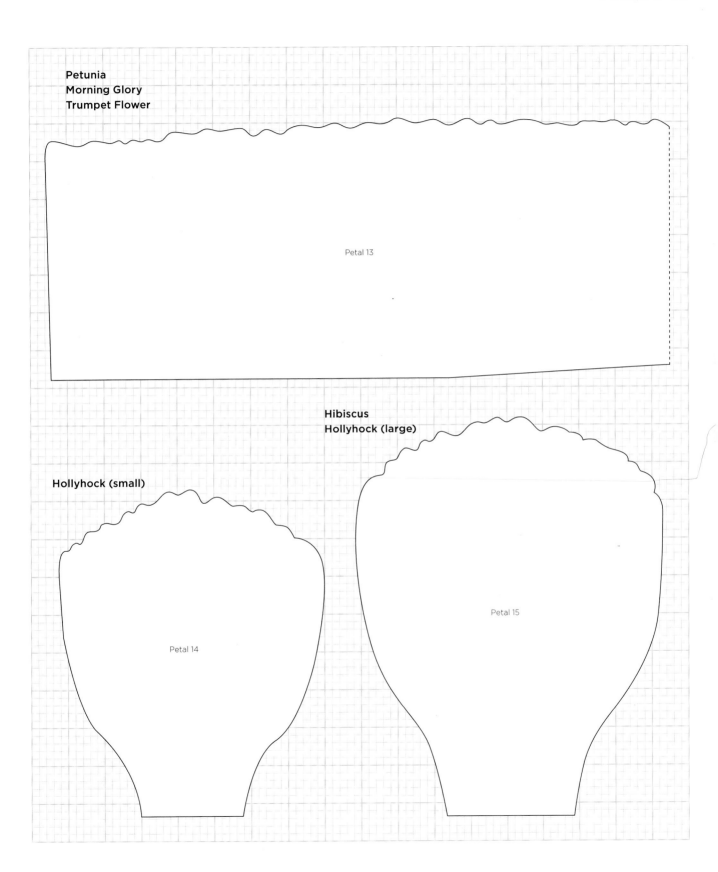

Petunia
Morning Glory
Trumpet Flower

Petal 13

Hibiscus
Hollyhock (large)

Hollyhock (small)

Petal 15

Petal 14

Templates

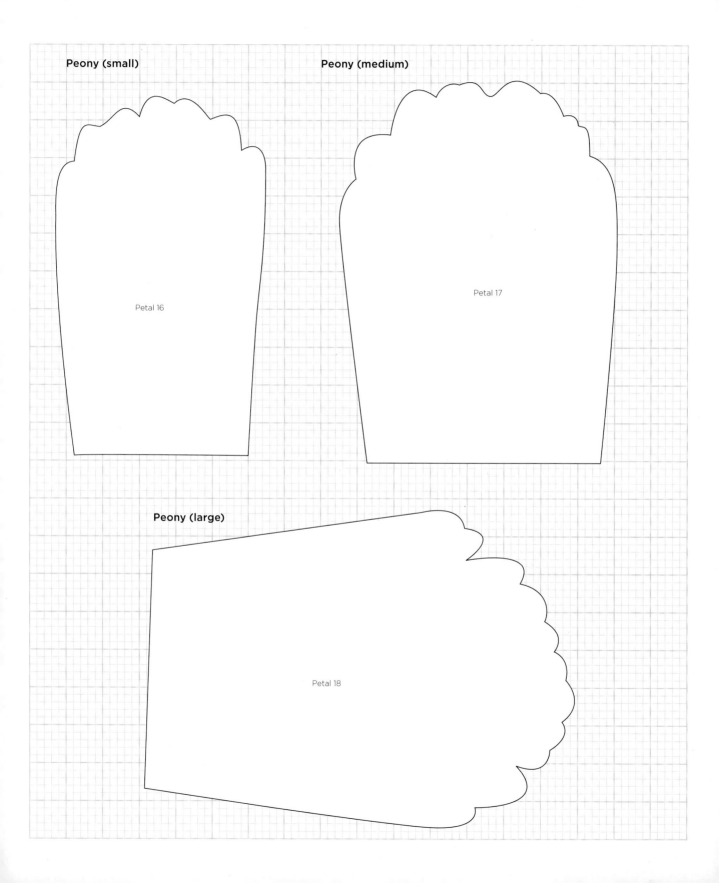

Peony (small)

Petal 16

Peony (medium)

Petal 17

Peony (large)

Petal 18

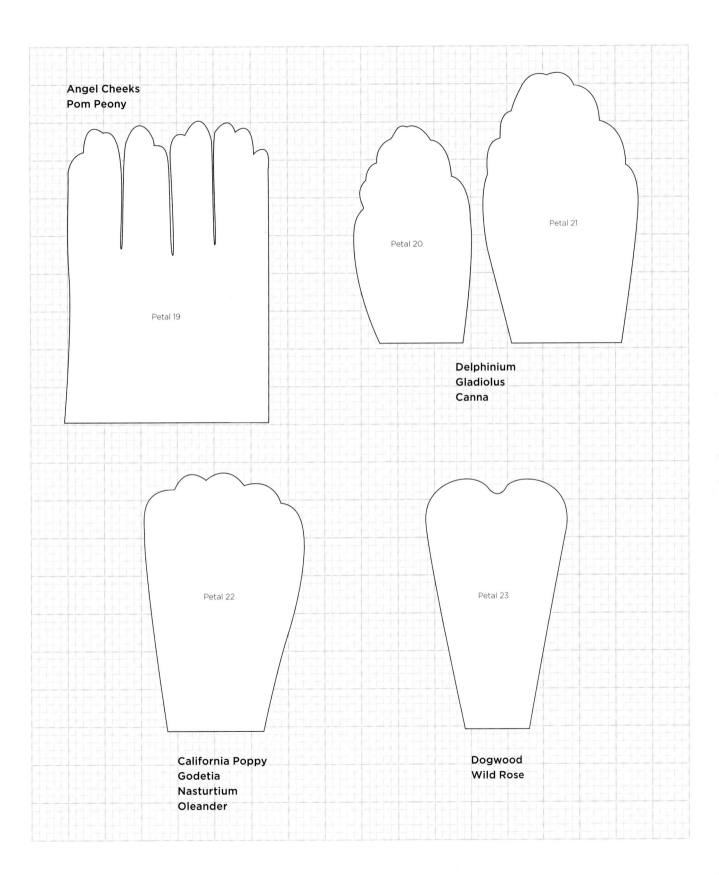

Angel Cheeks
Pom Peony

Petal 19

Petal 20

Petal 21

Delphinium
Gladiolus
Canna

Petal 22

Petal 23

California Poppy
Godetia
Nasturtium
Oleander

Dogwood
Wild Rose

Templates

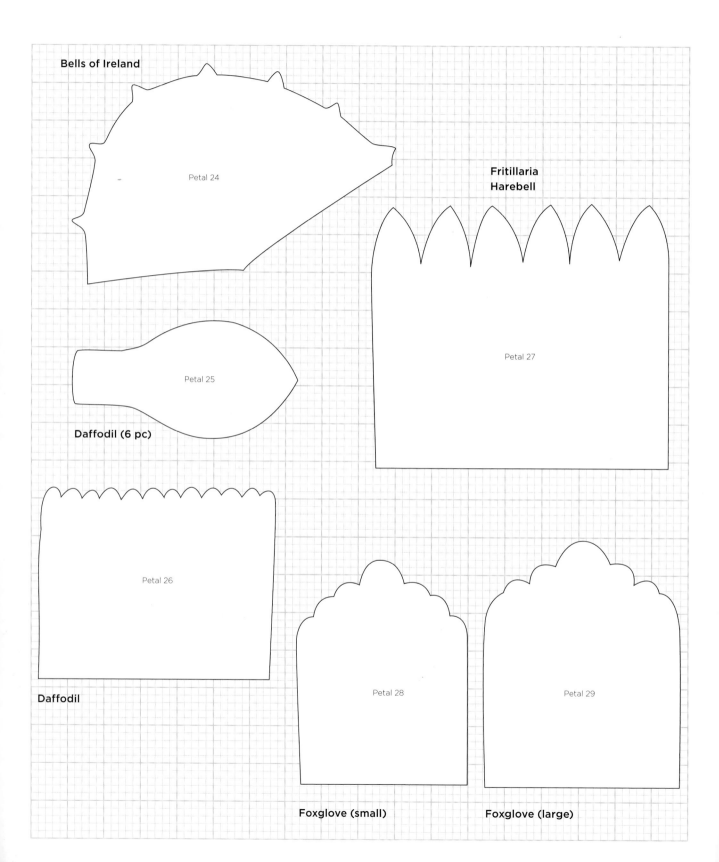

Bells of Ireland

Petal 24

Fritillaria
Harebell

Petal 27

Petal 25

Daffodil (6 pc)

Petal 26

Daffodil

Petal 28

Petal 29

Foxglove (small)

Foxglove (large)

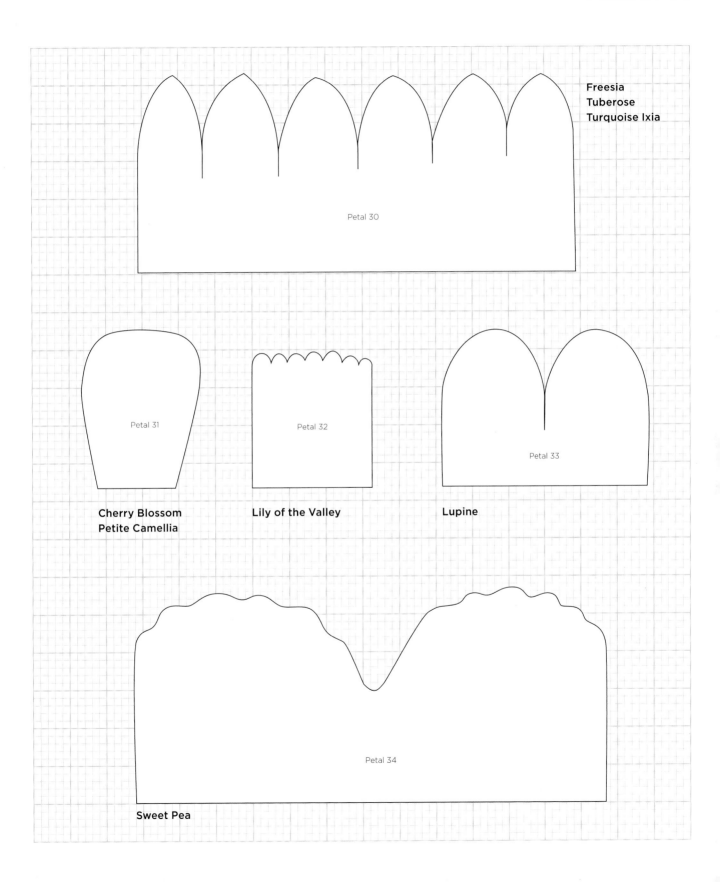

Freesia
Tuberose
Turquoise Ixia

Petal 30

Petal 31

Petal 32

Petal 33

Cherry Blossom
Petite Camellia

Lily of the Valley

Lupine

Petal 34

Sweet Pea

Templates

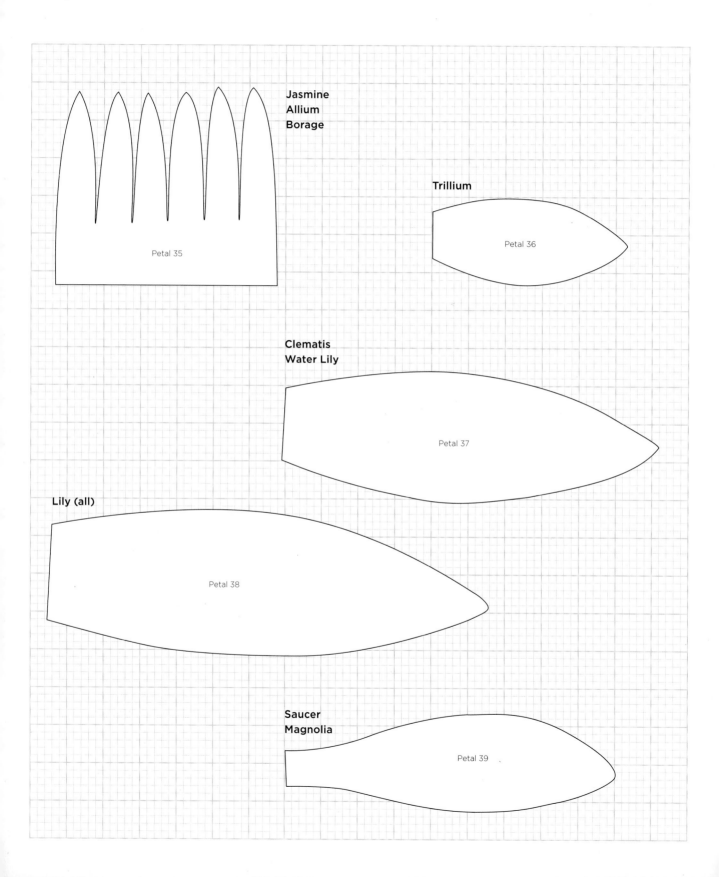

Jasmine
Allium
Borage

Petal 35

Trillium

Petal 36

Clematis
Water Lily

Petal 37

Lily (all)

Petal 38

Saucer
Magnolia

Petal 39

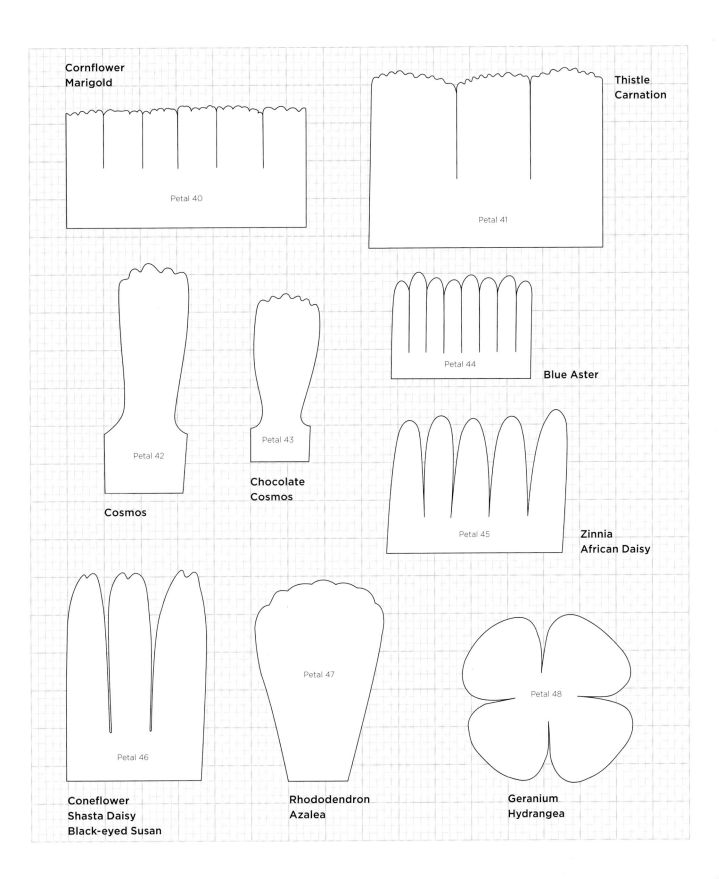

Cornflower
Marigold

Petal 40

Thistle
Carnation

Petal 41

Petal 42

Cosmos

Petal 43

Chocolate
Cosmos

Petal 44

Blue Aster

Petal 45

Zinnia
African Daisy

Petal 46

Coneflower
Shasta Daisy
Black-eyed Susan

Petal 47

Rhododendron
Azalea

Petal 48

Geranium
Hydrangea

Templates

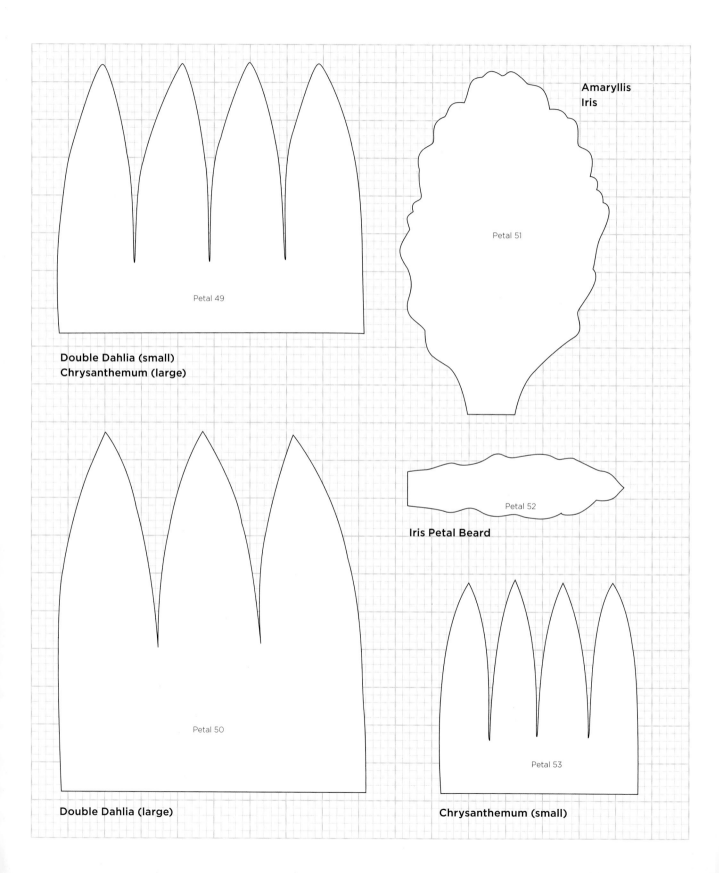

Petal 49

Double Dahlia (small)
Chrysanthemum (large)

Petal 50

Double Dahlia (large)

**Amaryllis
Iris**

Petal 51

Petal 52

Iris Petal Beard

Petal 53

Chrysanthemum (small)

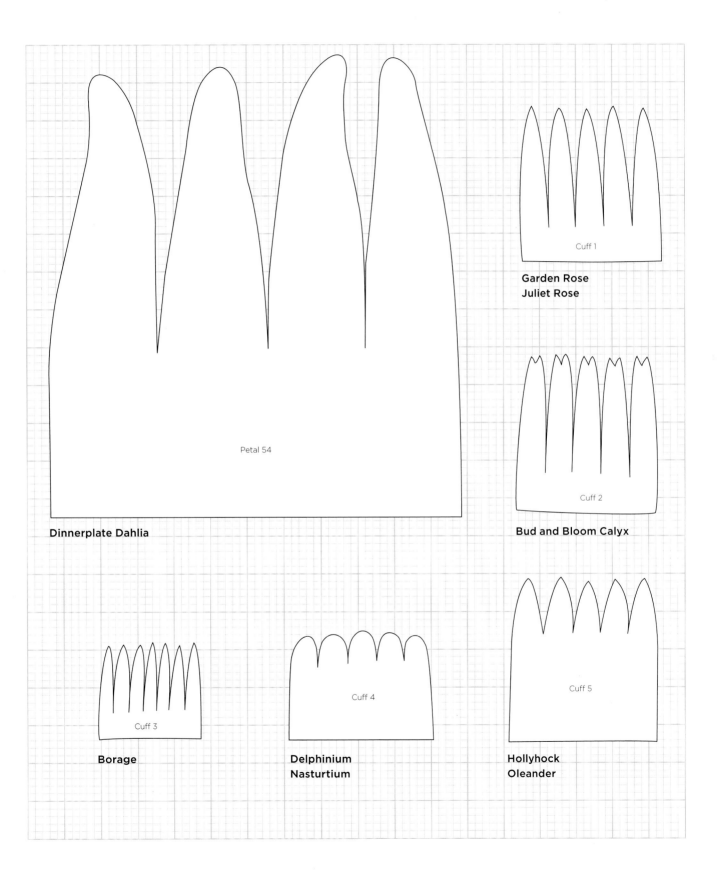

Petal 54

Dinnerplate Dahlia

Cuff 1

**Garden Rose
Juliet Rose**

Cuff 2

Bud and Bloom Calyx

Cuff 3

Borage

Cuff 4

**Delphinium
Nasturtium**

Cuff 5

**Hollyhock
Oleander**

Index